John Tyler

Gary May

John
Tyler

THE AMERICAN PRESIDENTS

ARTHUR M. SCHLESINGER, JR., AND SEAN WILENTZ

GENERAL EDITORS

Times Books

HENRY HOLT AND COMPANY, NEW YORK

Times Books
Henry Holt and Company, LLC
Publishers since 1866
175 Fifth Avenue
New York, New York 10010
www.henryholt.com

Henry Holt® is a registered trademark
of Henry Holt and Company, LLC.

Library of Congress Cataloging-in-Publication Data
May, Gary [date].
 John Tyler / Gary May.—1st ed.
  p. cm. — (The American presidents)
 Includes bibliographical references and index.
 ISBN-13: 978-0-8050-8238-8
 ISBN-10: 0-8050-8238-7
 1. Tyler, John, 1790–1862. 2. Presidents—United
States—Biography. 3. Vice-Presidents—United States—Biography.
4. Governors—Virginia—Biography. 5. Legislators—United States—Biography.
6. United States—Politics and government—1815–1861.
7. Virginia—Politics and government—1775–1865. I. Title.
 E397.M39 2008
 973.5'8092—dc22

 [B]   2008018131

Henry Holt books are available for special promotions and
premiums. For details contact: Director, Special Markets.

First Edition 2008

Printed in the United States of America

1 3 5 7 9 10 8 6 4 2

For Jacob Alan May,
with love

Contents

Editor's Note

THE AMERICAN PRESIDENCY

The president is the central player in the American political order. That would seem to contradict the intentions of the Founding Fathers. Remembering the horrid example of the British monarchy, they invented a separation of powers in order, as Justice Brandeis later put it, "to preclude the exercise of arbitrary power." Accordingly, they divided the government into three allegedly equal and coordinate branches—the executive, the legislative, and the judiciary.

But a system based on the tripartite separation of powers has an inherent tendency toward inertia and stalemate. One of the three branches must take the initiative if the system is to move. The executive branch alone is structurally capable of taking that initiative. The Founders must have sensed this when they accepted Alexander Hamilton's proposition in the Seventieth Federalist that "energy in the executive is a leading character in the definition of good government." They thus envisaged a strong president—but within an equally strong system of constitutional accountability. (The term *imperial presidency* arose in the 1970s to describe the situation when the balance between power and accountability is upset in favor of the executive.)

The American system of self-government thus comes to focus

in the presidency—"the vital place of action in the system," as Woodrow Wilson put it. Henry Adams, himself the great-grandson and grandson of presidents as well as the most brilliant of American historians, said that the American president "resembles the commander of a ship at sea. He must have a helm to grasp, a course to steer, a port to seek." The men in the White House (thus far only men, alas) in steering their chosen courses have shaped our destiny as a nation.

Biography offers an easy education in American history, rendering the past more human, more vivid, more intimate, more accessible, more connected to ourselves. Biography reminds us that presidents are not supermen. They are human beings too, worrying about decisions, attending to wives and children, juggling balls in the air, and putting on their pants one leg at a time. Indeed, as Emerson contended, "There is properly no history; only biography."

Presidents serve us as inspirations, and they also serve us as warnings. They provide bad examples as well as good. The nation, the Supreme Court has said, has "no right to expect that it will always have wise and humane rulers, sincerely attached to the principles of the Constitution. Wicked men, ambitious of power, with hatred of liberty and contempt of law, may fill the place once occupied by Washington and Lincoln."

The men in the White House express the ideals and the values, the frailties and the flaws, of the voters who send them there. It is altogether natural that we should want to know more about the virtues and the vices of the fellows we have elected to govern us. As we know more about them, we will know more about ourselves. The French political philosopher Joseph de Maistre said, "Every nation has the government it deserves."

At the start of the twenty-first century, forty-two men have made it to the Oval Office. (George W. Bush is counted our forty-third president, because Grover Cleveland, who served nonconsecutive terms, is counted twice.) Of the parade of presidents, a dozen or so lead the polls periodically conducted by historians and political scientists. What makes a great president?

Great presidents possess, or are possessed by, a vision of an ideal America. Their passion, as they grasp the helm, is to set the ship of state on the right course toward the port they seek. Great presidents also have a deep psychic connection with the needs, anxieties, dreams of people. "I do not believe," said Wilson, "that any man can lead who does not act . . . under the impulse of a profound sympathy with those whom he leads—a sympathy which is insight—an insight which is of the heart rather than of the intellect."

"All of our great presidents," said Franklin D. Roosevelt, "were leaders of thought at a time when certain ideas in the life of the nation had to be clarified." So Washington incarnated the idea of federal union, Jefferson and Jackson the idea of democracy, Lincoln union and freedom, Cleveland rugged honesty. Theodore Roosevelt and Wilson, said FDR, were both "moral leaders, each in his own way and his own time, who used the presidency as a pulpit."

To succeed, presidents not only must have a port to seek but they must convince Congress and the electorate that it is a port worth seeking. Politics in a democracy is ultimately an educational process, an adventure in persuasion and consent. Every president stands in Theodore Roosevelt's bully pulpit.

The greatest presidents in the scholars' rankings, Washington, Lincoln, and Franklin Roosevelt, were leaders who confronted and overcame the republic's greatest crises. Crisis widens presidential opportunities for bold and imaginative action. But it does not guarantee presidential greatness. The crisis of secession did not spur Buchanan or the crisis of depression spur Hoover to creative leadership. Their inadequacies in the face of crisis allowed Lincoln and the second Roosevelt to show the difference individuals make to history. Still, even in the absence of first-order crisis, forceful and persuasive presidents—Jefferson, Jackson, James K. Polk, Theodore Roosevelt, Harry Truman, John F. Kennedy, Ronald Reagan, George W. Bush—are able to impose their own priorities on the country.

The diverse drama of the presidency offers a fascinating set of tales. Biographies of American presidents constitute a chronicle of wisdom and folly, nobility and pettiness, courage and cunning, forth-rightness and deceit, quarrel and consensus. The turmoil perenni-ally swirling around the White House illuminates the heart of the American democracy.

It is the aim of the American Presidents series to present the grand panorama of our chief executives in volumes compact enough for the busy reader, lucid enough for the student, authori-tative enough for the scholar. Each volume offers a distillation of character and career. I hope that these lives will give readers some understanding of the pitfalls and potentialities of the presidency and also of the responsibilities of citizenship. Truman's famous sign—"The buck stops here"—tells only half the story. Citizens can-not escape the ultimate responsibility. It is in the voting booth, not on the presidential desk, that the buck finally stops.

—Arthur M. Schlesinger, Jr.

John Tyler

Prologue

The Instrument of a New Test

The two men on horseback, mud splattered and exhausted, finally reached the plantation home of Vice President John Tyler near Williamsburg, Virginia, at dawn on April 5, 1841. The younger, twenty-three-year-old Fletcher Webster, son of Secretary of State Daniel Webster and his father's chief clerk, carried the message that would change John Tyler's life. On behalf of the cabinet, Webster had come to inform Tyler that President William Henry Harrison was dead. For the first time in American history, a president had died in office and no one knew precisely what to do about it.

Webster and his colleague Robert Beale, the doorkeeper of the U.S. Senate, reined in their horses and quietly approached the front of the residence. Webster knocked loudly on the door, but there was no response; presumably Tyler and his family were asleep. Beale, used to controlling unruly senators, took his turn, pounding more vigorously. Soon sounds emerged from within and the door opened. The man who greeted them was tall and extremely thin, with a nose so prominent that people meeting him for the first time thought he resembled a classic Roman statesman. Still wearing his nightclothes (complete with cap), John Tyler shivered and his blue eyes blinked rapidly as they adjusted to the rising sun. Webster and Beale were invited inside, where Webster handed over the letter addressed to "John Tyler, Vice President of the United States." It read:

> Washington, April 4, 1841
>
> Sir:—It becomes our painful duty to inform you that William Henry Harrison, late President of the United States, has departed this life.
>
> This distressing event took place this day, at the President's mansion in this city, at thirty minutes before one in the morning.
>
> We lose no time in dispatching the chief clerk in the State Department as a special messenger to bear you these melancholy tidings.
>
> We have the honor to be with highest regard,
>
> Your obedient servants.

It was the first word Tyler received of Harrison's death, and curiously the letter did not declare that Tyler should hurry to Washington to assume the duties of the presidency.[1]

Tyler was startled but not surprised by the news. Indeed, months earlier, his good friend Littleton Tazewell told him that it was almost inevitable that he would become president, a prediction shared by many political observers. At sixty-eight, General William Henry Harrison was the oldest man ever elected president and many were surprised that the former hero of the Battle of Tippecanoe survived such a grueling campaign. "If Genl. Harrison lives, he will be President," Daniel Webster worried at the time. "His election is certain . . . if an all wise Providence shall spare his life." When a weary Harrison arrived in Washington for his inauguration in March 1841, he faced an onslaught of office seekers who harassed him at every turn. "They filled every room and defied eviction," wrote one observer. "The President opened a door, expecting to meet his Cabinet. The spoils men crushed about him. Soon [his] pockets were filled with their petitions, then his hat, then his arms;

and thus he staggered upstairs to revive himself with stimulants." Harrison complained that "they pursue me so closely that I can not even attend to the necessary functions of nature. . . . [They] will drive me mad!"

He escaped them by taking morning walks through the city streets and shopping in the capital's markets. One man noticed "an elderly gentleman dressed in black, and not remarkably well dressed, with a mild benignant countenance, a military air, but stooping a little, bowing to one, shaking hands with another, and cracking a joke with a third. And this man was William Henry Harrison, the President of this great empire . . . unattended and unconscious of the dignity of his position—the man among men, the sun of the political firmament. People say what they will about the naked simplicity of republican institutions. It was a sublime spectacle."[2]

During a stroll in late March, Harrison was drenched by a sudden downpour. He developed a cold, which soon became pneumonia. A team of physicians did everything they could to save him; Harrison was "bled, blistered, cupped, leached, massaged, poked" and forced to swallow ipecac, opium, and brandy, as well as "mixtures containing crude petroleum and Virginia snakeweed." The cure proved worse than the disease and contributed to the president's death. His final words, according to a physician in attendance, were directed to Tyler, whom Harrison, in his delirium, thought was by his bed: "Sir, I wish you to understand the true principles of government—I wish them carried out, nothing more."[3]

Tyler had left Washington soon after taking his oath of office on March 4. He did not attend any of Harrison's inaugural festivities and nobody noticed his absence. As vice president, his only responsibilities were presiding over the Senate and breaking a tie vote if necessary, and the Senate was in recess until June. Like the vice presidents before him, he expected to play no major role in government. His immediate predecessor, Richard M. Johnson, had so much free time that he opened a tavern in Kentucky and enraged his fellow Southerners by consorting with a young black woman believed to be his third wife. Tyler was happily married to a Virginia belle, had had eight children, and ran a plantation; these aristocratic activities would fill his hours, rather than his duties in Washington.[4]

But then Harrison became ill. Tyler did not personally witness the president's deteriorating health, but he did receive reports from Washington. "Near all the doctors in the city are in attendance upon him, and the general impression seems to be that he will not survive the attack which is one of violent pleurisy," wrote Tyler's friend James Lyons. Lyons expected that it would soon be announced that "Genl. Harrison is no more." His predictions may have given Tyler the time to consider what he would do should he suddenly become president.[5]

After Harrison died, his cabinet met hurriedly at one o'clock in the morning to discuss how to officially announce the death and to plan the funeral. They drafted the letter to Tyler and sent Webster and Beale on the 230-mile trip to Williamsburg. In the Whig cabinet's view, Tyler was merely "the Vice President, acting as president."[6]

Letter in hand, Tyler gently awakened his wife and children and informed them of the news. Then he dressed, had breakfast, and conferred with his friend the law professor Beverley Tucker, who urged him to announce immediately that he would only complete Harrison's unfinished term and not seek the presidency in 1844. The diplomatic Tyler listened politely but refused to eliminate any options before taking office. By 7:00 a.m. Tyler and his son John Jr. (who often acted as his personal secretary) set out for Washington, taking every form of conveyance then available—horse, steamboat, and train—arriving there just before dawn on Tuesday, April 6, "a remarkable record for speed."[7] They set up headquarters at Brown's Indian Queen Hotel and Tyler arranged to meet soon with Harrison's cabinet.

It was obvious to Tyler that the capital was deep in mourning for the dead president. Flags flew at half-staff; government and private offices closed their doors; and the "President's House" and many private residences were draped in black crepe. "For the first time since the formation of the Government, the people have been called upon to mourn the demise of their Chief Magistrate," observed one journalist. "Every heart seems bowed down with grief— every countenance marked with sadness. His death is felt to be a national calamity."

For many, the tragedy of Harrison's death was compounded by Tyler's ascension. Two former presidents of different parties were especially upset. Andrew Jackson, a Democrat, called Tyler "an imbecile in the Executive Chair." Jackson's nemesis, Whig congressman John Quincy Adams, thought Tyler "a political sectarian of the slave driving, Virginian, Jeffersonian school . . . with all the interests and passions and vices of slavery rooted in his moral and political constitution." For Adams, Harrison's death brought to the presidency "a man never thought for it by anybody." Like many of his fellow Whigs, Adams dismissed Tyler as merely an "Acting President" temporarily exercising the powers of the office without lawfully occupying it.[8]

Others believed that Tyler's mild, patrician manner meant that he would be easily controlled. "I fear that Tyler is such a poor weeping willow of a creature," the editor Francis P. Blair told Jackson, "that he will resign all to the audacious depravity of the political black-leg." That depraved black-leg was Senator Henry Clay of Kentucky, perennial presidential aspirant and leader of the congressional Whigs. The Whigs believed in a weak presidency dominated by a strong Congress, and Clay planned to govern the country from the Senate. Harrison tried to resist but had proved no match for the wily Clay. With Tyler widely viewed as but "a flash-in-the-pan" whose main "defect" was a lack of "moral firmness," Clay hoped to continue his domination until he could win the presidency in 1844. But Tyler, within hours of his arrival in Washington, showed the Whig cabinet that he was stronger than they had expected.

The new president was aware that his actions would create precedents that would bind his successors. Indeed, if Tyler did nothing else during his years as president, this first decision would secure his place in history. Regarding presidential succession, the Constitution was vague and ambivalent. Article II, Section 1 stated, "In case of the removal of the President from Office, or of his Death, Resignation, or Inability to discharge the Powers and Duties of the said office, the Same shall devolve on the Vice President." But to what did the words "the same" refer? The office, or just the powers and duties which the vice president would temporarily discharge until a new president was elected? The Twelfth Amendment, ratified in 1804, only added to the confusion. It created a system by which electors voted for candidates clearly designated president and vice president and stated that should the chief executive die the "Vice-President shall act as President"—not become president. The records of the Constitutional Convention were not available to Tyler and his contemporaries; works by noted lawyers and jurists were equivocal, some arguing that the founders intended that the vice president assume both the office and its powers, and others disagreeing.[9]

Tyler tended to interpret the Constitution narrowly and in the past had been critical of Andrew Jackson's aggressive presidency. But now he was willing to be guided more by circumstance than by principles. His colleagues had judged him by his quiet and passive manner but, in fact, Tyler was fiercely ambitious. None of the previous vice presidents had held so many political offices—state legislator, governor, U.S. congressman, senator, and vice president—and Tyler saw himself as the successor not simply of William Henry Harrison but of the other Virginia presidents—Washington, Jefferson, Madison, and Monroe.

With Harrison's cabinet assembled, Tyler declared that he was not the vice president acting as president but the president of the United States, possessing both the office and its full powers. When Secretary of State Daniel Webster explained that President Harrison and his cabinet cast equal votes in reaching decisions and that the majority ruled, Tyler announced that he could not accept such a practice. "I beg your pardon, gentlemen," he said. "I am very glad to have in my cabinet such able statesmen as you have proved yourself to be. And I shall be pleased to avail myself of your counsel and advice. But I can never consent to being dictated to. I am the President and I shall be responsible for my administration." If they found this unacceptable, they should resign, although he preferred that they remain at their posts for the present. No one challenged Tyler or submitted a resignation. Webster then suggested that, given the uncertainty caused by Harrison's death, it might be wise if Tyler took the oath of office. He agreed, though he personally did not think it necessary. A short time later, William Branch, the chief justice of the United States Circuit Court of the District of Columbia, administered the oath and Tyler formally became the tenth president of the United States, and, at fifty-one, the youngest man ever to hold the office.[10]

Tyler must have been pleased with his first day as president. He established a precedent that would affect the future of the presidency long after he left office and he had managed to keep Harrison's government intact, which provided stability at a critical time. But he also knew that his actions would inevitably trigger reactions not to his liking. His decision to retain Harrison's cabinet, while momentarily necessary, was problematic. Tyler did not have "a sincere friend" in the cabinet and he knew the dangers this posed. "[I am] surrounded by Clay men, Webster men, anti-Masons, original Harrisonians, Old Whigs and new Whigs," he wrote a friend, "each jealous of the others, and all struggling for the offices." To a former Senate colleague, William C. Rives, he noted: "I am under Providence made the instrument of a new test which is for the first time to be applied to our institutions. The experiment is to be made at the moment when the country is agitated by conflicting views of public policy, and when the spirit of faction is most likely to exist. Under these circumstances, the devolvement upon me of this high office is peculiarly embarrassing. In the administration of the government, I shall act upon the principles which I have all along espoused . . . derived from the teachings of Jefferson and Madison. [M]y reliance will be placed on the virtue and intelligence of the people."[11]

1

The High Road to Fame

The young John Tyler met the revered Thomas Jefferson, founding father and former president of the republic, on October 21, 1809, when Jefferson came to dine at the Tyler home. For Jefferson, recently retired from the presidency after the election of his protégé James Madison, the visit to Richmond was something of a homecoming, although perhaps not a pleasant one. Jefferson would be dining at "The Palace," the residence of the governor of Virginia, Judge John Tyler. When Jefferson had occupied the office from 1779 to 1781, he had been forced to flee the invading British army and was charged with cowardice. Still, Jefferson probably looked forward to a reunion with Governor Tyler, whom he had known since they were law students nearly forty years earlier.

Governor Tyler asked his nineteen-year-old son John to supervise the arrangements for the meal. The boy was happy to provide "a good dinner" for the Sage of Monticello. John deemed Mr. Jefferson a splendid raconteur and listened attentively to his tales of the Revolution and his views on the current state of the nation. As dessert approached, "a door flew open, and a Negro servant appeared, bearing, with both hands raised high above his head, a smoking dish of plum-pudding," Lyon G. Tyler, the family historian, later wrote. "Making a grand flourish, the servant deposited it before Governor Tyler. Scarcely had he withdrawn before another door flew open, and an attendant, dressed exactly like the first, was seen bearing another plum-pudding, equally hot, which at a grave nod from young John, he placed before Mr. Jefferson." The governor thought that perhaps John had overdone it, remarking: "*Two* plum-puddings John; two plum puddings! Why, this is rather extraordinary!" "Yes, sir," John replied, "it *is extraordinary*." He then rose from the table, bowed to Jefferson, and said, "it is an *extraordinary occasion*." A memorable event certainly, but dining with such a distinguished figure was not unusual for young John Tyler; it was typical of his life as a Virginia aristocrat.[1]

. . .

John Tyler was born at Greenway, a beautiful plantation estate located on twelve hundred acres of fertile soil in Charles City County, Virginia, on March 29, 1790. He was the sixth of eventually eight children (and the second son) of John and Mary Armistead Tyler. Little is known about Tyler's early years (most of his personal papers were destroyed during the Civil War) but his biographers believe that his greatest influences were his father and the intellectual and physical environment in which Tyler was reared.

His father, Judge John Tyler, as he came to be known, was a formidable figure "of strong convictions and prejudices, both of which he expressed with utter fearlessness." Although the judge's father (also named John) served as marshal of the colony's vice admiralty courts, which strictly enforced Britain's control over Virginia's trade with other nations, the son became a committed revolutionary. In 1765, nineteen-year-old John Tyler and his friend Thomas Jefferson joined the crowd at the Virginia House of Burgesses to hear Patrick Henry attack the Crown and proudly proclaim, "If this be treason, make the most of it." Tyler's "soul caught fire at the sound of Henry's voice," and he attacked George III in newspaper articles and pamphlets, much to Marshal Tyler's displeasure ("Ah! John," said father to son, "they will hang you yet for a rebel; they will hang you yet.")[2]

Despite his rebellious spirit, Judge Tyler followed a traditional path to prominence. He attended the College of William and Mary and studied law with a distinguished Williamsburg attorney before marrying Mary Armistead, the daughter of a wealthy Virginia planter. He then began his career in earnest, first winning election to the Virginia House of Delegates, in which he served from 1778 to 1786, half the time as Speaker. For a decade, from 1788 to 1798, he was judge of Virginia's General Court. In 1808, he was elected governor of Virginia and finally, prior to his death in 1813, won appointment as a U.S. district court judge. His life was spent serving the Old Dominion. For Judge Tyler, Virginia was the true mother country.[3]

Despite a long and busy career, Judge Tyler was an attentive and loving father to his children, especially after Mary died in 1797, when John was seven years old. A housekeeper named Mrs. Bagby was hired to help fill the void left by the death, and John's four older sisters also comforted him. Plantation life at Greenway, with its crops of corn, wheat, and tobacco to cultivate, some forty slaves to care for and supervise, animals to raise, and Thoroughbred horses to ride, likely provided distractions from John's boyhood grief. Because of his father's position, there was also an endless stream of visitors: distinguished jurists, poets, and politicians such as Patrick Henry and James Monroe caused a flurry of excitement. But it was Judge Tyler who became the center of John's world. According to biographer Robert Seager, he "absorbed in toto the political, social, and economic views of his distinguished father."

The father would gather his children under "the grand old willow that caressed the house," tell tales of his exciting youth, read stories with the flair of a professional actor, and serenade them with his violin. He would often turn to the subject of politics. Although he was proud of the role he had played in the Revolution, Judge Tyler was not happy with the government that had been created and had opposed ratification of the Constitution. "[I]t never entered my head that we should quit liberty and throw ourselves into the hands of an energetic government," he wrote in 1788. "When I consider the Constitution in all its parts, I cannot but dread its operation. It contains a variety of powers too dangerous to be vested in any set of men whatsoever."[4]

For the Tylers, Virginia was paramount. Not only was it the wealthiest, most populous, and most influential colony and then state, its sons led the fight for independence, wrote its most sacred documents, then dominated the new federal government. John Tyler grew up with a collection of heroes unsurpassed in America's history—Washington, Jefferson, Madison, Monroe; George Wythe, who taught Jefferson the law and signed the Declaration of Independence; Patrick Henry, the revolutionary firebrand, governor of Virginia, and Tyler family friend; Edmund Randolph, George Washington's attorney general and secretary of state. Four of the new nation's first five presidents and Chief Justice John Marshall were Virginians. It was the Old Dominion's finest age, as historian Susan Dunn noted, though Tyler would be the last Virginian to be president, a reflection of the state's mid-nineteenth-century economic and political decline.[5]

Virginia was unique as well. Unlike other states, its economy was almost solely agrarian and based on slave labor. Its people believed that they had created a separate civilization, a "virtuous republic based on noble yeomen tilling the fertile earth and expanding into the infinite wilderness to prolong the agrarian idyll." Virginia republicanism—based on states' rights, limited government, a strict interpretation of the Constitution, and the preservation of slavery—was John Tyler's personal, political, and intellectual inheritance.[6]

John's education in republicanism was fostered in 1802 when the twelve-year-old prepared to enter the College of William and Mary (which is, after Harvard, the oldest institution of higher learning in America). It was a natural choice; both his grandfather and father, like most Southern patricians, had gone there, as had Thomas Jefferson. Those who knew John Tyler at the college described him as a quiet, serious boy who preferred writing poetry and playing the violin to the rough-and-tumble. Physically, he was "very slight . . . his long, thin patrician face dominated by the high cheekbones and the prominent nose. . . . His lips were thin and tight, his dark brown hair was silken." Illnesses—intestinal pain and chronic diarrhea or respiratory ailments—were constant companions.[7]

However weak his body, John excelled at school. Ancient history, poetry, and the works of William Shakespeare were his favorite subjects. He learned Latin and Greek and found Adam Smith's *Wealth of Nations*, with its call for trade unrestricted by tariffs or government interference, consistent with his emerging political philosophy. He memorized passages from Smith's writings that would later be incorporated into his presidential messages. His father's frequent letters provided paternal wisdom: "Ignorance is the mother of superstition, whose offspring is slavery, which begets a tyranny in the end." However, he noted one serious deficiency in John's education—penmanship. "I am mortified to find no improvement in your handwriting," he informed him; "neither do you conduct your lines straight, which makes your letters look too abominable. It is an easy thing to correct this fault, and unless you do so, how can you be fit for lawbusiness [sic] of every description?" (Taking his father's admonition seriously, John improved his handwriting, and would eventually express similar concern over his own children's penmanship. "A young lady should take particular pains to write well and neatly," Tyler wrote his daughter Mary in 1827, "since a female cannot be excused for slovenliness in any respect.")[8]

At William and Mary, John was influenced by his favorite teacher, the Reverend Bishop James Madison, the college president and a second cousin to the future fourth president of the United States. A dynamic speaker who dazzled thousands of students during his more than three decades as the school's intellectual and spiritual leader, Madison established what historian Edward Crapol called the William and Mary "school of empire and national destiny," a theological justification for American expansion. God, Madison argued in his sermons and essays, had created the new nation to spread republican virtue and enlightenment throughout the world. Tyler was converted. Madison's philosophy, Tyler said later, was "indelibly impressed upon my heart and mind."[9]

John Tyler graduated from William and Mary in 1807, a few months after his seventeenth birthday. He was one of four students selected to deliver his class's commencement address. Judge Tyler recommended education as a subject for his "senior oration," but his son took the topic a bit further than anticipated. Remembering that Judge Tyler always hoped that his daughters would someday be as well educated as his sons, John spoke about the need for "Female Education." All but one of the listeners who gathered in Williamsburg's Bruton Parish Church to hear his talk called it "the best commencement oration" they had ever heard. The exception was Bishop Madison, who was enraged, "gesticulating wildly with his hands and walking cane" while his favorite student declaimed heresy. John ignored his protest and finished speaking amid a roar of applause.[10]

Like his father before him, John Tyler found his calling in public service. There was no more noble and necessary profession. "[G]ood and able Men had better govern than be gover'd," the Judge believed, "since 'tis possible, indeed highly probable, that if the able and good withdraw themselves from Society, the venal and ignorant will succeed." Tyler chose the law because, he said, it was "the high road to fame." His father was his first mentor, followed by his cousin Samuel Tyler; in 1809, when his father became governor, John went to work with a William and Mary alumnus, Edmund Randolph, the former U.S. attorney general. Tyler loved the law but not the way Randolph, a Federalist, interpreted it. "He proposed a supreme national government," a sickened Tyler recalled, "with a supreme executive, a supreme legislature, and a supreme judiciary, and a power in Congress to veto state laws." Nothing could have been farther from the republican ideal.[11]

Tyler finished his legal studies in two years, at age nineteen. Although he had not yet reached the age required for admission to the bar, he was admitted, no doubt because of his excellent record and family connections. He quickly made a name for himself and a comfortable income as an attorney specializing in criminal law.

Having the governor as his father must have attracted some clients, but he was also considered one of the most dynamic courtroom "performers" of his day, able "to play on the emotions of jurors as though they were strings of his violin."[12]

Given Tyler's profession and social standing in Charles City County, it is not surprising that he won election to the Virginia House of Delegates in 1811, when he was just twenty-one. Instead of quietly learning from his more experienced colleagues and refraining from bold action, Tyler, barely a month after assuming office in December 1811, took on Virginia's two U.S. senators.

In the previous session, the statehouse had instructed Senators William Branch Giles and Richard Brent to oppose the rechartering of the Bank of the United States, which many states' rights republicans, Tyler among them, considered unconstitutional. When they ignored the "sacred" custom of legislative instruction and voted in favor of the bank, Tyler was furious. Without seeking the advice of more senior delegates, he introduced three resolutions censuring Giles and Brent, despite each man's long record of public service. Their "conduct," Tyler said, was "incompatible with the principles of a Republican government." In his view, Giles and Brent "did cease to be the true and legitimate representatives of this State." No records exist to indicate how Tyler's colleagues reacted, but they must have been upset because the resolutions were sent to a committee, which softened their inflammatory language. Still, the final draft embodied Tyler's opinion that U.S. senators must follow the legislature's instructions, and the Virginia House approved it overwhelmingly. Tyler's victory did not entirely satisfy him, however. Almost a year later, in December 1812, Tyler voted to table the reading of a message from Senator Giles, an attempt to silence his opponent.[13]

Tyler was moving steadily along his road to fame, but he lacked one important criterion of a successful politician: a wealthy and distinguished wife. At a graduation party in 1809, he had met Letitia Christian, a lovely young woman with brown hair and brown eyes who was the daughter of Percilla and Robert Christian of Cedar Grove, a plantation estate in New Kent County, Virginia. The Christians were a well-known and affluent family, and the fact that Robert served in the Virginia House of Delegates as a Federalist seems not to have bothered Tyler or his father. Letitia had all the talents expected of her gender in that age—she ably supervised the house slaves and played piano and sang—though she was said to be "quiet" and "reserved." Little is known about their four-year engagement, but it seems to have been "calm" and "undemonstrative"; Tyler admitted that it was not until just before their wedding day that he summoned the courage to kiss her hand. Yet it was not a mere marriage of convenience. Writing to her in December 1812, Tyler told Letitia that her "happiness is now my only object, and whether I float or sink in the stream of fortune, you may be assured of this, that I shall never cease to love you."[14]

His happiness was diminished in January 1813, when Judge Tyler contracted pneumonia and died. To officially mourn the passing of the former governor, Virginia state legislators wore black crepe badges on their arms for thirty days, an honor only previously accorded to President George Washington. Judge Spencer Roane, Patrick Henry's son-in-law, remembered the judge as "a friend to the rights of mankind, and a thorough Republican in his principles and manners." "Upon me," his son John wrote, "he conferred the name which he bore, and I shall be well content to reflect but the shadow of his patriotism, intelligence, and worth." Judge Tyler was buried beside his wife in the family plot at Greenway.[15]

Less than three months later, on his twenty-third birthday, John Tyler married Letitia Christian at the Cedar Grove plantation. He had no wedding jitters, he later explained to a friend. "I had really calculated on experiencing a tremor on the near approach of the day; but I believe that I am so much of the old man already as to feel less dismay at a change of situation, than the greater part of those my age," he wrote. "I have reflected deeply on the consequences, and whether prosperity smiles or adversity frowns, I believe that I shall keep from sinking." The newlyweds moved to

Mons-Sacer, a five-hundred-acre farm located on Greenway Plantation.[16]

. . .

In the first summer of his marriage, John Tyler joined his countrymen in what they called the "Second War of Independence" from
Great Britain, and his experience proved that sometimes adversity
smiles as well as frowns. In May 1813, two thousand British troops
attacked Hampton, Virginia, quickly defeating the city's militia.
The conquerors released their French prisoners of war and allowed them to go on a rampage. "Every horror was committed
with impunity," observed one British officer, "rape, murder, pillage
and not a man was punished!" Just as disturbing to Virginians was
how successful the British were in recruiting slaves to join the
fight. Many feared that the Capitol at Richmond would be the next
to suffer.[17]

With the Old Dominion under assault, Tyler left his bride and
joined the Charles City Rifles, a ragtag local militia. Perhaps because he represented Charles City County in the House of Delegates or simply because he had a famous name, Tyler was
appointed captain. He tried to turn the group of inexperienced
farmers into a fighting force but was not successful. Regardless, the
Rifles joined the larger Fifty-second Regiment of the state militia
and marched to Williamsburg, where they waited for battle while
housed in a dormitory on the William and Mary campus. One
night, the men were awakened with a report that British troops
were in the area. They rushed to action only to fall down the stairs
into an undignified pile. Victory in battle could save them from this
embarrassment, but when they reached the grounds there was not
a single British soldier in sight. The report was just a rumor of war.
In later years, Tyler would laugh about his "distinguished military
services during the War of 1812," but his political opponents often
poked fun at Captain Tyler's misadventures. When the British left
Hampton, the militiamen returned home, pride hurt but at least
alive—and able to rejoice in America's surprising victory in 1815.

Tyler's experience in the war did not stall his career. He won annual elections to the House of Delegates four more times, once overwhelmingly defeating seven opponents. In 1815, he was elected to the executive council, the body that advised the governor. The following year, when U.S. representative John Clopton, who stood for Richmond, died, Tyler entered the race, narrowly defeating Virginia Speaker of the House Andrew Stevenson in a special election. At twenty-six, he became one of the youngest congressmen in America.[18]

Upon arriving in Washington on December 17, 1816, Tyler discovered a city still showing the ravages of the British invasion. The Capitol was destroyed and members of the House and Senate displaced. The president's house, plundered and set ablaze by British troops, was uninhabitable and undergoing repairs; nine more months would pass before the building was deemed safe enough for occupation. There were other problems that could not be blamed on the British. The city's streets were mostly unpaved; dust in dry times and mud in wet made travel along Pennsylvania Avenue treacherous. Cows and hogs roamed freely, competing for space on walkways with congressmen. Swampland brewed malaria and other infectious diseases. The capital was "the most forlorn and melancholy place . . . I was ever in," said one foreign visitor.[19]

In January, Congress convened in a hastily constructed brick building, which quickly became known as the "Old Brick Capitol." Tyler and his fellow representatives met on the building's second floor, where they sat on "ordinary wooden seats" while their counterparts in the Senate occupied the first floor, cushioned by rich upholstery. Despite the plain surroundings, the House's distinguished members left Tyler starstruck. "As a debater and writer," Tyler noted, South Carolina's John C. Calhoun "had few, if any superiors." Daniel Webster of Massachusetts was already showing the "broad and expansive intellect" that would make him a legend in the Senate. The eccentric John Randolph of Virginia came to the House "booted and spurred" and carrying a whip that some thought he might use against his rivals. Though sometimes besotted by

drink and opium, Randolph reminded Tyler of a "comet . . . blaz-
ing through the heavens, throwing off scintillations of wit and genius, until his course in debate was paved with stars." Towering
over all was Kentucky's Henry Clay, Speaker of the House. Brilliant, urbane, decisive, and eloquent, "nature had bestowed upon
him in profusion her gifts," Tyler wrote. "He added to an intellect
of the highest order a commanding person, and his voice and ges-
ture and manner were those best calculated to sway the action of a
popular assembly. Had he lived in the time of Pericles, his name
would have found a place of high eminence in Athenian history."[20]

Clay had a vision to match his abilities. America's dismal military performance in the War of 1812 shaped him profoundly. The
war suggested that the nation must change if it wished to survive. It
must build a strong army and navy to defend itself from further
British aggression and foster an independent and self-sufficient
economy. The future lay in manufacturing and industry. This "market revolution" required a system of internal improvements—
roads, canals, and turnpikes that only a strong central government
was capable of financing and constructing. Most of these programs
were reminiscent of Alexander Hamilton's economic vision for
America, but now even Republicans, including President Madison,
could see the wisdom in it.

Clay was the most forceful advocate for this new "American
System." His plans were expansive. He wanted a revitalized Bank
of the United States to provide fiscal order; government-supported
internal improvements and public works; more tariffs like the Tariff of 1816 to protect American goods from foreign competition;
the creation of a ten-thousand-man army; and more. Since the
South had long opposed a strong central government, Clay expected that the old Republicans would balk at the new policies but
begged them to understand that "the force of circumstances and
the lights of experience" required such actions.[21]

The new congressman from Richmond had to choose between
following Clay's lead or remaining committed to states' rights. Tyler
stayed true to the Republican faith, which placed him at odds with

the Speaker. In his maiden speech to the House on January 18, he pledged to represent his constituents, to listen to their views rather than just pursue "popular favor." He likened popularity to "a coquette, the more you woo her, the more she is apt to elude your embrace." "Popular clamour" would not move him, he asserted; he would respond solely to "the voice of a majority of the people, distinctly ascertained and plainly expressed." When a bill designed to create a fund to support Clay's internal improvements was introduced in the House, Tyler voted against it because he thought that such public works insulted his constituents, presuming that Virginia was "in so poor a condition as to require a *charitable* donation from Congress." Philosophically, he also noted that the Constitution did not explicitly give the federal government the power to build roads and canals.[22]

In late 1818, Tyler was given a chance to closely examine the operations of the one institution that epitomized Clay's American System: the Second Bank of the United States. The bank had been set up in March 1816, but had failed to provide the economic stability its advocates promised. Instead, a "bank mania" ensued—state banks proliferated, speculation was rife, and corruption widespread. At the same time, the end of the Napoleonic Wars and other events reduced the demand for both manufactured goods and agricultural staples, and triggered the first great depression in America's history. It was most deeply felt in the South and the West. "[Virginia] is in a state of unparalleled distress," Thomas Jefferson wrote. "Our produce is now selling at market for one third of its price. . . . I fear local insurrections against these horrible sacrifices of property." The House responded by appointing John Tyler and four other congressmen to a special committee to examine what role the bank might have played in either causing or failing to prevent the country's economic collapse.[23]

Tyler spent the last months of 1818 on the investigation. The team traveled through a bitter winter storm to the bank's headquarters in Philadelphia and immersed themselves in its voluminous and complex records. It was long, tedious work. To demonstrate their seriousness, they rejected many of the dinner invitations they received from local dignitaries and only dined out on the occasional Sunday. Tyler wrote his brother-in-law Dr. Henry Curtis: "I certainly . . . never encountered more labor. To be placed in a situation of novelty and great responsibility; to have to wade through innumerable and huge folios . . . ; to have money calculations to make; and perplex one's self with all the seeming mysteries of bank terms, operations, and exchanges—the strongest mind becomes relaxed and the imagination sickens and almost expires."[24]

In January 1819, Tyler and his committee presented their findings, including more than a hundred pages of documents, to Congress. They found the bank directors guilty of mismanagement and violations of the bank's charter. In a series of speeches, Tyler attacked the bank's "long catalogue of crime" and called for its abolition and the removal of its revenues to more dependable state banks.

For those who knew Tyler's record and Republican philosophy, the charges were not a surprise, but there had been some optimism that the American System was poised to prevail over states' rights. Even Madison and Monroe recognized that their worldview required readjustment to fit the times. Tyler remained more orthodox; while appreciating that at some future moment "manufacturing and industry would become essential ingredients . . . for national greatness," they should not be hurried into practice. Tyler considered the bank "to be the original sin against the Constitution," likening it to a deadly "serpent." The old Hamiltonians and the new nationalists like Clay had promised "boundless wealth. . . . [T]he banks, like Midas, were to turn everything into gold." But that "dream" was now dead. Instead of wealth there was only "penury" and "bankruptcy," "sorrows" not "blessings," "shadow" not "substance," "rags and paper" not "gold." Only the tillers of the soil were truly virtuous and "our Republic can only be preserved by a strict adherence to virtue," he declared. "It is our duty . . . to put down this first instance of detected corruption, and thereby to preserve ourselves from its contamination."

Tyler's view, however, did not find favor. The bank's supporters rallied to its cause, which received a boost when the U.S. Supreme Court upheld the bank's legality in *McCulloch v. Maryland*. Only minor adjustments in its operations were made and the Second Bank of the United States survived its first battle.[25]

• • •

An even more serious challenge to Tyler's principles, his political future, and the Southern way of life awaited him. In February 1819, Congress was considering admitting the Missouri territory into the Union as a slave state. On Saturday, February 13, New York congressman James Tallmadge Jr. offered an amendment to prohibit the further importation of slaves into Missouri and to eventually free those already there. The Southern response was immediately explosive. Georgia congressman Thomas W. Cobb leaped to his feet and, shaking his fist at Tallmadge, yelled: "If you persist, the Union will be dissolved. You have kindled a fire which all the waters of the ocean cannot put out, which seas of blood can only extinguish." "Let it come!" Tallmadge replied with equal venom. The amendment passed the House (Tyler voted no) but it failed in the Senate.

The crisis entered a second stage during the next congressional session in 1820. By then, Missouri's status had become a toxic national issue. The precarious balance between slave and free states was at risk, and each section feared the worst about the other: Southern interests thought the move was a Northern attempt to end Virginia's control of the presidency as well as the South's future control of Congress if slave states predominated. "Missouri is the only word ever repeated here by politicians," Tyler informed Henry Curtis. "You have no possible idea of the excitement that prevails. . . . Men talk of a dissolution of the Union with perfect nonchalance and indifference." "God has given us Missouri," cried John Randolph, "and the devil will not take it from us." In the battle to come, Tyler defended the embattled South. "I cannot and will not yield one inch of ground," he declared.[26]

Tyler was an ambivalent slave owner. He believed that the "peculiar institution" was inherently evil, but the Southern way of life, his own life, could not exist without it: forty slaves lived and worked at Greenway and made his financial success possible. Tyler was physically sickened by the most barbaric aspects of slavery, such as Washington City's slave market, where blacks were examined like cattle and auctioned to the highest bidder. But while he was always a "slave owner with a conscience," meaning that he did not allow his slaves to be whipped by cruel overseers, he kept his slaves forever in bondage. Despite his efforts to mitigate its brutality Tyler, like other slave masters, could not prosper let alone survive without slavery. In historian Walter Johnson's words, they were all "men made out of slaves." Tyler's son Lyon, a historian and president of the College of William and Mary, put it more charitably: "Mr. Tyler . . . deplored slavery; but it was here without his fault or that of his contemporaries, and he, like the best patriots of the Revolution, would tolerate no officious interference from without."[27]

Illness prevented Tyler from contributing to the congressional debate until February 17, 1820. By that time, a series of compromises were emerging. Maine, then a part of northern Massachusetts, would be admitted as a free state, while slavery would be permitted in Missouri. This would allow the Union to be equally divided between slave and free states. But at the same time, slavery would be forbidden from taking root in the Louisiana Purchase (excepting Missouri) north of 36'30". When Tyler finally spoke before the House, he blamed the North for precipitating the crisis, misunderstanding and violating the Constitution, and failing to comprehend that the spread of slavery actually benefited both the slave and the nation at large. Pointing to Article IV, Section 2 of the Constitution, which stipulated that those slaves who escaped their masters must be returned, Tyler argued that a Southerner's right to own slaves was guaranteed; this attempt to restrict the spread of slavery would open the gates for the government to seize at will the property of any citizen. Further, because the Louisiana Purchase Territory had been bought from "a common purse" of Southern as well as Northern money, preventing the future citizens living in the area from owning slaves was unjust. The North intended to rob the South of its fair share of this national bounty.

If slavery was indeed a "dark cloud," the way to eliminate it, Tyler asserted, was to allow it "to diffuse" until it became a gentle "summer's cloud," just as former presidents Jefferson and Madison advocated. Limiting slavery would only lead to its concentration in Southern states, breeding "unrest as well as repression." Allowing it to spread alleviated such tension and made eventual abolition more likely. A flourishing trade in slaves would also make them more valuable to their owners, who would be less inclined to physically harm them. In opposing the developing Missouri Compromise, Tyler concluded, "[Y]ou ameliorate the condition of the slave [and] you add much to the prospects of emancipation, and the total extinction of slavery." Those who rejected the proposed bill would receive the "blessings" of their countrymen. Those who did not would earn "the deepest curses of posterity." Several more weeks of haggling ensued before the Senate and the House approved Clay's compromise, and President James Monroe signed it into law on March 6, 1820.[28]

Congress's action depressed Tyler. Years later, as the Civil War approached, he looked back on the Compromise of 1820 and recalled: "I believed it to be unconstitutional. I believed it to be . . . the opening of the Pandora's Box, which would let out upon us all the present evils which have gathered over the land. I never would have yielded to the Missouri Compromise. I would have died in my shoes, suffered any sort of punishment you could have inflicted upon me, before I would have [supported] it." This new defeat, coming after his failure to destroy the Second Bank of the United States, suggested that the future looked especially bleak for Tyler and his fellow Virginians. In December 1820, he decided not to seek reelection. "[T]he truth is that I can no longer do good here," he wrote Henry Curtis. "I stand in a decided minority, and to waste words on an obstinate majority is utterly useless and vain."[29]

Personal issues also persuaded Tyler it was time to go. He was now the father of three young children, all under five years, with another expected within a few months, and he and Letitia wanted more (eventually they would have eight). "My children will soon be treading on my heels, and it will require no common exertions to . . . educate them," observed Tyler. His once thriving law practice—he was earning two thousand dollars a year prior to coming to Washington—had declined significantly, and his congressional salary was embarrassingly small. "In truth, the really valuable business has passed into other hands," he noted. In short, he needed to make some money and soon. "Most important," he told Dr. Curtis, was "the duty" he owed his family.

Then there was his health, which he called "very precarious." Almost a year earlier, on January 31, 1819, he suffered an acute illness that still baffles medical historians. That morning, while on his way to the House, he felt "a disagreeable sensation" in his head that intensified once he arrived in the building. He hurried outside and the feeling spread throughout his body; it made his "limbs, tongue, etc. almost useless." He was helped into a carriage and returned to his boardinghouse, where he was examined by a physician. Following the therapies of the day, he was "bled" and given "purgative medicines." The doctor's diagnosis was "a diseased stomach."[30]

Since we have only Tyler's description of his symptoms and no other records, it is impossible to determine definitively what caused the attack. Botulism seems most likely, given the generally unsanitary conditions in Washington, and "stale fish" was frequently served at Tyler's boardinghouse. However, a mild case of Guillain-Barré syndrome or even myasthenia gravis cannot be entirely ruled out because of the later recurrences of his illness.[31] Tyler was able to return to his work within a few days but continued to complain of feeling "a glow in my face and over the whole system, which is often followed by debility with pains in my neck and arms." He was still not fully recovered in July 1821: "For a week at a time I feel as well as ever," he wrote Curtis, "but then comes the fit again, and I suffer severely. . . . The disorder not only affects my body, but often my mind. My ideas become confused, and my memory bad."[32]

On January 15, 1821, he informed his constituents that "the state of my health renders it necessary and proper that I should decline the honor of a re-election to Congress." Thanking the freeholders of his district for giving him the honor of serving them, he did, however, hold open the possibility of a return to public life: "I go, fellow citizens into retirement; but should occasion require it, and destiny permit, I shall ever be ready to contribute my mite to the advancement of the country's happiness." As much as he looked forward to "those enjoyments in the bosom of my family and in the circle of my friends," at almost thirty-one he was determined to continue to fight those "dangerous principles which have . . . sprung up among us."[33]

2

The Sentinel

Tyler's retirement from politics was brief. He enjoyed his reunion with his wife and children, but to his surprise he quickly discovered that he no longer liked practicing law. Once he had enjoyed the drama of defending desperate criminals at trial, but now most of his clients were members of his extended family—which brought him no money—or the local government, which gave him little satisfaction.[1]

His frustrations exploded one day when a man named Thomas Macon, whom he had roughly cross-examined in court, came to complain about his treatment. "Mr. Tyler," Macon said, "you have taken with me a very unjustifiable liberty." Tyler denied doing so but commented on Macon's poor courtroom demeanor. Incensed, Macon replied: "You have not acted the part of a gentleman, sir." For a man of Tyler's class and status, there were few greater insults, and Tyler suddenly hit Macon. A fistfight ensued; Macon struck Tyler with his riding crop, but Tyler managed to seize it, returning the blows. The two were eventually separated by spectators, but Tyler thought he was the victor. He happily told friends that Macon's face was so badly bruised in the fight that despite the passage of time, "his appearance even now gives evidence of it."[2]

The life of a gentleman farmer also disappointed him. In the best of times, Virginians, as Susan Dunn noted, were more skilled at statecraft than farming. An overreliance on slave labor and "single crop farming," an exhausted soil, and poor management made a farmer's existence far from idyllic. Tyler's return to the land in 1821 coincided with an especially bad period for wheat, his main crop. "The wheat never perhaps promised less to the husbandman than now," noted the *Richmond Enquirer*.[3]

Politics provided an escape from this domestic boredom. In April 1823, Tyler decided to seek election to one of two vacancies in the Virginia legislature. He won. Over his following two years in the state capital, he resisted change. When a more open, democratic system of choosing presidential electors was introduced, he dissented vocally—but lost. Reformers at the College of William and Mary, which had fallen on hard times, recommended a move from Williamsburg to Richmond; Tyler opposed it. Education, he believed, flourished "in the shade and delighted in the stillness of solitude," rather than in the jangling disharmony of the city. He mounted a campaign to defeat relocation and succeeded. It was clear to his colleagues that his years in Washington had not changed him—he remained "an undeviating Republican." Then in 1825, Tyler was elected governor, the office once held by Thomas Jefferson and his own beloved father. But it was an insignificant post, designed by the men of 1776 who opposed executive power. Tyler accomplished little; he recommended a public school system for all Virginia children, but left it to the legislature, where the real power resided, to act. Invariably, it did not, and Tyler appeared most content with the status quo.[4]

Yet he was not without ambition, as well as a bit of luck. By 1827, Senator John Randolph had become an embarrassment to the citizens of the Old Dominion. Particularly troubling were Randolph's bizarre personal habits. One critic charged that "he dressed and undressed himself in the Senate Chamber," unacceptable behavior by a gentleman anywhere, let alone one representing Virginia. Randolph was "a royal nuisance," who "had to be handled with infinite care, for he was a wicked debater with a sharp and nasty tongue."[5] His current targets were President John Quincy Adams and Secretary of State Henry Clay. On March 30, 1826, in "perhaps the most offensive speech ever heard in that body," Randolph called Adams and Clay a "combination of the Puritan and the blackleg." Clay, who for years had been an object of Randolph's barbs, had enough and the following day challenged him to a duel. Randolph accepted. On the morning of April 8, they exchanged shots on the Virginia side of the Potomac, because Randolph insisted on shedding his blood only on home soil. Neither was injured, but Randolph's reputation was finally shattered. His enemies at home looked for a more genteel politician to oppose him in the next election and their choice was Governor John Tyler.

Tyler publicly expressed his continuing admiration for Senator Randolph while privately allowing the anti-Randolph forces to place his name in nomination. On January 13, 1827, Tyler defeated Randolph by five votes. Randolph took the whole thing in stride; when the two later ran into each other at Richmond's racetrack, Randolph extended his hand, saying: "How is your Excellency? And when I say your Excellency, I mean your Excellency." At thirty-six, Tyler was the U.S. senator from Virginia.[6]

Tyler had the position but not the funds to support himself in the Capitol. "My monied affairs are all out of sorts," he wrote Henry Curtis, "so much so that I scarcely know how I shall reach Washington." Financially strapped, he decided to sell his most disposable property: Ann Eliza, a favored house slave among the Tyler family. At first, Tyler tried to place her with a good family who would not harm her. He offered her to his brother-in-law, but Curtis was not interested. He asked Curtis to solicit his neighbors, but none wanted her. A few weeks before he was to be sworn in, Tyler decided that if a sale between friends or acquaintances was not possible, "then the better way would be to put her in the wagon and send her directly to the Hubbard's . . . for public auction. Her sale has become indispensably necessary to meet the demands of my trip." Eliza never returned to Greenway, so she was likely sold, probably at auction, which would mean that Tyler began his Senate career with monies generated by the sale of a human being.[7]

. . .

Tyler's return to Washington in December 1827 coincided with a democratic political revolution led by Andrew Jackson. In background and temperament, Tyler and Jackson were completely different, reflecting the changing nature of American leadership. Tyler had been born and bred in comfort; Jackson's parents were poor Irish immigrants who had settled in the Carolina backcountry to become subsistence farmers. Tyler's father was warm and supportive; Jackson's father was killed in an accident shortly before Jackson's birth, in 1767. The Revolutionary War launched Judge Tyler's career. Jackson was not so fortunate: the war destroyed his family and it almost cost him his life too, when a British officer's sword cut into his head, leaving him scarred for life. His eldest brother, Hugh, died following the Battle of Stono Ferry in 1779; his brother Robert fell to scarlet fever; and his mother died of cholera while nursing American prisoners of war.[8]

While Tyler's rise to prominence was steady, assisted by his affluent connections, Jackson's was solitary, swift, and often violent. Although poorly educated, Jackson read law and became a successful lawyer and businessman in Tennessee. Whereas Tyler engaged in his single fistfight with Macon, Jackson, quick-tempered and chronically angry, "brawled and quarreled incessantly, coolly and deliberately killed a man in a duel, fought others with cane, fists, and gun." Jackson catapulted to the Senate at age thirty, but left a year later to become a justice on Tennessee's Supreme Court. His victory at the Battle of New Orleans in 1815 made "Old Hickory" a national hero. Three years later President Monroe authorized him to pursue marauding Seminoles into Spanish Florida. Seizing the area, he found two British "spies," who were charged with inciting the Indians. After a hurried military trial, they were executed, though Jackson had not asked for the government's permission. His behavior was criticized in Congress by Tyler, among others. "I demand to know who was authorized, under the Constitution to have declared [this] war—Congress or the General?" Tyler cried. "We live in a land where the only rule of our conduct is the law."[9]

Tyler's warnings were ignored, and Jackson's popularity skyrocketed. Jackson's methods may have been harsh, his supporters admitted, but he had paved the way for American control of Florida. "Old and young speak of him with rapture," a pro-Jackson newspaper claimed. But when friends urged Jackson to seek the presidency, he demurred, remarking: "I know what I am fit for. I can command a body of men in a rough way; but I'm not fit to be President."[10]

Then the financial Panic of 1819 and the sectional strife created by the Missouri Compromise, among other events, nurtured the popular animosity against Washington insiders. This benefited the war hero, who by 1824 concluded that he was ready to be president. It was a crowded field: his chief opponents were Secretary of State John Quincy Adams; Speaker of the House Henry Clay; and Secretary of War William Crawford (who was in the race despite poor health). Jackson won 41.3 percent of the popular vote. But without a majority in the electoral college, the election was thrown into the House of Representatives, where the three candidates with the most electoral votes—Jackson, Adams, and Crawford—scrambled for votes.[11]

Speaker Clay was heartsick over his defeat. If only the paralyzed Crawford had dropped out, Clay—the master of the House—might have been able to shift things his way. Now he was forced to choose between the lesser of the two great evils: Jackson or Adams. Clay detested Adams but believed a Jackson presidency would be "the greatest misfortune that could befall the country." And since Adams shared with him similar views on economic issues, Clay backed Adams, who, in the so-called corrupt bargain, won the electoral majority and the presidency. President-elect Adams appointed Clay to be his secretary of state—the post from which the previous three presidents had ascended.[12]

For John Tyler, the election was a victory without joy. He originally supported Secretary Crawford—the states' rights candidate—but his illness led Tyler to look elsewhere. Both Henry Clay and John C. Calhoun advocated the hated American System, so they were unacceptable. Andrew Jackson, whom Tyler feared since the Florida adventurism, personified almost everything Tyler hated about the new frontier politics. "[N]o government can last for any length of time, in consonance with public liberty, without checks and balances," he later said. "Without them we rush into anarchy, or seek repose in the arms of monarchy. We can neither trust King Numbers or King One with unlimited power. Both play the despot." Jackson conjured the threat of despotic rule supported by the illiterate masses. For Tyler nothing was worse, so he supported the nationalist Adams. Tyler believed that the fact that Adams won the presidency with only 30 percent of the popular vote would limit the president's worst ideological predilections.[13]

Tyler was proved wrong. The president, in his first Annual Message to Congress, in 1825, asked for the enactment of new nationalist economic and educational programs, including vast internal improvements and the creation of a national university and astronomical observatory. None were to Tyler's liking. "From the moment of seeing that message," Tyler explained, "I stood distinctly opposed to this administration." He stood ready to defend his sacred principles, becoming "a zealot" on behalf of "liberty and the Constitution." He was not alone. Jacksonians swept the off-year election of 1826, winning control of Congress, and they set out to destroy the president and prepare for Old Hickory's election in 1828. Their plan, conceived chiefly by New York senator Martin Van Buren, the master political strategist of his day, was to recreate the old Jeffersonian alliance of Southern planters and Northern Republicans to do battle against Federalism, reincarnated in the person of John Quincy Adams.[14]

Their chief tool was a new tariff bill designed to build support for Jackson in the mid-Atlantic, South, and West while hurting Adams in New England, where he was strong. The Jackson men thought they could not lose: if the tariff became law, their candidate's chances of victory would be increased; if Adams vetoed the bill, it would be used as a potent issue against him with New England manufacturers. Tyler understood the political machinations behind the bill but in the end voted against "that curse to the whole South." When the tariff passed both houses and Adams signed the "Tariff of Abominations" into law, it planted the seeds for one of the great crises in American history.[15]

. . .

The presidential contest of 1828 must have reminded Tyler of 1824. Tyler's top choice, New York governor DeWitt Clinton, had constructed the extraordinary Erie Canal with state rather than federal resources, proving that the country could develop internal improvements without ceding state autonomy. But Clinton did not wish to run and supported Jackson. Once again, Tyler was left without a candidate, confronted with choosing between the hated Adams and the frightening Jackson. Swallowing his fears, he picked Jackson. To his brother-in-law Henry Curtis, Tyler admitted that he was "most earnestly solicitous for Jackson's success. . . . Every day that passes inspires me with the strong hope that his administration will be characterized by . . . Republican simplicity."[16]

Despite his private optimism, Tyler was publicly silent during the campaign. But he must not have liked the contenders' ungentlemanly tactics in a campaign that "began in the gutter and remained there." Jackson's wife, Rachel, received special vilification. The truth itself was politically embarrassing: she had left her abusive husband Lewis Robards for Jackson before marrying him, both believing, incorrectly as it turned out, that Robards had divorced her. Now Clay's scandalmongers asked, "Ought a convicted adulteress and her paramour husband to be placed in the highest offices of this free and Christian land?"[17] Jackson's propagandists responded by attacking Secretary Clay and President Adams with equal venom. Besides advertising rumors about the "corrupt bargain," Clay was called a "traitor" for having consorted with Aaron

Burr, while Adams was considered a monarchist with "royal extrav-
agances." Yet nothing could stop the Jackson bandwagon, and he
won the presidency easily with 56 percent of the popular vote.[18]

Tyler further warmed to Jackson after he entered the White
House. He observed that Jackson "seemed to me to lay aside the
royal diadem. . . . All satisfied me that I stood in the presence of an
old-fashioned republican." Tyler was especially pleased when, in
May 1830, the president vetoed the Maysville Road bill, preventing
the use of federal funds to construct a Kentucky highway, a program of internal improvements. Jackson's veto "is hailed with un-
bounded delight by the strict constructionists," Tyler rejoiced, "and
the two houses of Congress resound with his praise." To his friend
Littleton Tazewell, Tyler wrote that the veto "is good as a first step,
and greatly raises my hopes and confidence."

Actually, Jackson was not, as Tyler believed, "a strict constructionist." By various means, the president was seeking "a middle
path" between the Adams-Clay nationalists and radical Southerners like his vice president, John C. Calhoun, who coveted the presidency. For example, in July 1832, Jackson signed into law a new
tariff, an effort to amend the 1828 Tariff of Abominations by low-
ering its rates. Northerners, whose manufacturers needed such protection, favored it, but it did not satisfy the Southerners. Tyler
called it "an unmixed pill of bitterness," a sign that materialism was
taking over the nation. "Man cannot worship God and Mammon,"
Tyler told the Senate during an exhausting three-hour speech. "If
you would preserve the political temple pure and undefiled it can
only be done by expelling the moneychangers and getting back to
the worship of our fathers." Finding middle ground was proving
difficult.[19]

Still, Tyler's admiration for Jackson intensified that year when
the Second Bank of the United States again became the center of
controversy. Given Jackson's animus toward monopolistic, antidem-
ocratic institutions, it is likely that he would have eventually gone
after the bank, but the involvement of its current director, Nicholas
Biddle, in anti-Jackson politics made a showdown inevitable. Jackson

had learned that bank branches in Kentucky and Louisiana contributed to Adams's coffers during the 1828 campaign, and the bank's headquarters in Philadelphia bursted with anti-Jackson feeling. Biddle was known to buy support from congressmen, including the eminent Daniel Webster, making the bank "an enormous financial and political power." The new president had wanted to take on the bank early in his first term, but his closest political advisors urged him to wait.[20]

In December 1831, hoping to head off the simmering conflict, Treasury Secretary Louis McLane, a friend of both Biddle and the bank, forged a compromise in which the bank would reform certain of its practices in order to secure the president's approval of another charter. Jackson was amenable to the deal. It would reform America's economic system and eliminate the national debt, which was of crucial importance to him. But Jackson wanted one important assurance—that the rechartering not occur prior to the 1832 election.

When McLane issued a report urging that the bank be rechartered, antibank journalists, including editor Francis Blair, one of Jackson's closest advisors, learned of it and howled. Later that month, the National Republican Party nominated Henry Clay for president and quickly expressed its support for Biddle and the bank. The party issued a statement predicting that a reelected Jackson would abolish the bank, and Clay, now Kentucky's U.S. senator, hoped to use the bank issue to win the presidency. Clay convinced Biddle to immediately seek a renewed charter. After Biddle remarked that Jackson would almost surely veto the bill, the arrogant Clay replied, "Should Jackson veto it, I will veto him!"[21]

Early in 1832, a rechartering bill that left the bank's powers generally unchanged made its way through Congress. The House Ways and Means Committee supported the bill, spurring Jackson to write that the bank had become "a hydra of corruption, so dangerous to our liberties by its corrupting influences everywhere, and not the least in the Congress." For his part, Tyler continued in his hatred of the bank. He became Jackson's ally in the Senate, opposing the bill and supporting every amendment designed to defeat it. The bank's policies, Tyler proclaimed, turned America into "a nation of usurers." The Senate passed the measure, by only eight votes, as did the House, by a significantly wider margin. Biddle, adding insult to injury, invited his supporters to join him in a celebration so noisy that "it would reach the ears of the President."[22]

Biddle's defiance enraged Jackson. He vetoed the bill and issued an explosive explanation of his decision. Previously, presidential vetoes were rare and occurred because the president deemed a law unconstitutional. Jackson pushed far beyond this to a president's prerogative on economic, political, and social factors and framed the issue to put the office of the presidency clearly on the side of the people. "It is to be regretted that the rich and powerful too often bend the acts of government to their selfish purposes," Jackson said. "[Therefore], the humble members of society—the farmers, mechanics, and laborers—who have neither the time nor the means of securing like favors to themselves, have a right to complain of the injustices of their Government."[23]

Tyler supported Jackson's veto, but while he believed that "money is the great corrupter," he had little confidence in "the humble members of society." He disliked class warfare, and Jackson's expansive view of presidential power worried him. Yet he could never vote for Clay. "Clay stands no chance," he wrote. "Jackson is invincible." To Tyler's delight, Jackson won the veto fight and, with it, reelection.[24]

· · ·

As the Jacksonians celebrated their victory, a political storm was forming in South Carolina. It had started in 1828, when Vice President John C. Calhoun, angry and depressed over the passage of the Tariff of Abominations, returned home to brood about the future of his country. And he was good at brooding. An English visitor to the Senate called him "the cast-iron man, who looks as if he had never been born and never could be extinguished." "I hold the duties of life to be greater than life itself," Calhoun noted. His most

sacred obligation was to the Palmetto State, which he believed suffered under all tariffs, new and old.[25]

Calhoun's solution to the tariff threat was nullification, a right
that he believed belonged to every state. The Union was essentially
a compact of states that had agreed to form a government to which
it delegated certain powers. If a state considered a federal law unconstitutional, it could declare it null and void, and fight its enforcement. At the request of the South Carolina legislature,
Calhoun codified his thinking in an unsigned document, called the
"Exposition and Protest," which was widely distributed throughout
the state. Four years later, it became a guide to action. In the presidential election, the state's electors had rejected both Jackson and
Clay in favor of Virginia governor John Floyd. On November 19,
1832, a special state convention issued an Ordinance of Nullification, proclaiming the Tariff of Abominations and its more recent
progeny "null, void and no law"; the ordinance would go into effect
on February 1, 1833.[26]

When news of South Carolina's challenge reached Jackson, he
lashed out. While Congress had been granted the right by the Constitution to enact tariffs, nullification was quite another matter. Calhoun was demented, he told a friend; the rebellion's leaders would
be arrested, their "wickedness, madness and folly . . . and the delu-
sion of their followers in the attempt to destroy themselves and our
union has not its parallel in the history of the world." In a dramatic
proclamation on December 10, he rejected the state's philosophical case: nullification was "incompatible with the existence of the
Union, contradicted expressly by the letter of the Constitution,
unauthorized by its spirit, inconsistent with every principle on
which it was founded, and destructive of the great object for which
it was formed." Furthermore, it was the president, not Congress,
who represented the people. He bluntly informed South Carolina
that "disunion by armed force is treason," and its people would pay
"dreadful consequences."[27]

Tyler stepped in to resolve the crisis. He did so by turning to the
one man he felt might devise a way out of this nightmare—Henry

Clay. Clay "received [him] cordially. . . . He saw the danger." Flatter-
ing the recently defeated presidential contender, Tyler persuaded
Clay of "the true glory which he had it in his power now to acquire"
by finding a solution that both North and South could support. Tyler
claimed that Clay hesitated, asserting that others should assume the
leadership, but then agreed. Since Clay was already privately dis-
cussing a possible compromise prior to seeing Tyler, it is likely that
the roguish Clay was having a bit of fun at Tyler's expense.[28]

Regardless, Clay needed little convincing. His entire political career had built to this moment, and a success might wipe away the
stain of his recent debacle, increase his popularity in the South,
and win him the presidency in 1836. Clay told Tyler about his plan
to continue the present tariff system until 1840, when it would be
altered significantly so that all tariff duties would be equal and collected only to provide the revenue necessary for the government to
function. If the South could give him "time," Clay said, the "principle" of protecting one special region would die. "Time is of little
importance to us," Tyler replied. The South had long suffered under the tariff system. But he agreed to discuss Clay's plan with
other Southerners who wished to avoid war.[29]

Tyler next met with Governor John Floyd. "Consult in the
strictest confidence with those around you and let me have your
views," he told Floyd. "Bear in mind that the principle of protection
is to be utterly abandoned and the wound inflicted on the Constitution thereby to be healed." Tyler argued that Clay's plan had
something for everyone—the North would enjoy the fruits of protection for a few more years, then it would be gone and the South
freed of its scourge. "When we talk of reconcilement and a restora-
tion of peace," he concluded, "would it not be better to have peace
de facto and embrace in true brotherly affection?" Clay's genius
had nearly convinced Tyler "that the battle is fought and won. My
fears for the union are rapidly dissipating."

Tyler's hopes for a settlement were premature. Although the administration did support a bill designed to reduce the tariff, each
side seemed bent on a military confrontation. Some nullifiers, calling

themselves the Whigs and their enemies the Tories, believed that they were battling King Andrew I, as their patriotic ancestors had fought King George III. When a South Carolina congressman met with the president and asked him if there was anything he could tell his constituents, Jackson replied: "Please give my compliments to my friends in your state and say to them, that if a single drop of blood shall be shed there in opposition to the laws of the United States, I will hang the first man I can lay my hand on engaged in such treasonable conduct, upon the first tree I can reach." South Carolina's governor called for military volunteers, while Jackson continued to build up his forces. He wrote, "The Union must be preserved. . . . I will die with the Union."[30]

Tyler found himself in an especially difficult position. He would soon face reelection. The standoff had shocked his beloved Virginia, arousing unionists in the West and nullifiers in the East. An opponent who espoused nullification might well defeat him. Like many politicians who want to retain their jobs, he struggled to find a middle ground that would appeal to both sides. The result was a sword's-blade stance that distinguished him from both Jackson and Calhoun. As a strict constructionist, Tyler rejected nullification because the Constitution nowhere gave that power to the people. But as a states' rights man, he believed that the states were sovereign and therefore had the right to secede from the Union if that was their choice.

He became increasingly troubled by Jackson's expansion of presidential power and began to call the White House "the Palace." During Jackson's first term, Tyler had twice criticized the president for abuses of office. "There is already the spice of monarchy in the presidential office," he had told the Senate. When Tyler learned that Jackson planned to ask for congressional authorization to use force against South Carolina's "rebellion," he turned decisively against the president. Jackson had "deceived" him, Tyler told a friend. "His Proclamation has swept away all the barriers of the Constitution, and given us, in place of the Federal government . . . a consolidated military despotism. . . . I tremble for South Carolina."[31]

On January 16, 1833, Jackson formally submitted his "Force Bill" to the Senate. Ten days later, the Virginia legislature proclaimed its support of state sovereignty and called the president's action unconstitutional. This spurred Tyler to take a public stand. On February 6, he spoke out against the "Bloody Bill." Tyler was an extremely able speaker; Jefferson Davis, for one, thought him "the most felicitous among the orators I have known." The visitors' gallery was more crowded than usual, perhaps because Tyler's political future was uncertain—in just nine days, Virginia's General Assembly would either reelect Tyler or choose another. He did not disappoint his audience. It was perhaps the most emotional speech he had ever delivered. The issues at stake, his son later wrote, "aroused all the energies of his soul."

Tyler began by expressing his hope that a peaceful settlement could be achieved by means of the compromise he had discussed with Clay. "The manufacturers desire time," he said. "Give them time, ample time. If they will come down to the revenue standard and abandon the protective policy, I would allow them full time." Certainly this approach was preferable to a war against South Carolina. "You level her town and cities in the dust; you clothe her daughters in mourning, and make helpless orphans of her rising sons;—where then is your glory?" he implored. "Glory comes not from the blood of slaughtered brethren. Gracious God!" his voice choked. . . . "Whither has the genius of America fled? We have had darker days than the present, and that genius has saved us."

The Union should not buckle under the "pernicious doctrine" of nationalism, Tyler asserted. "Everything, Mr. President, is running into nationality. You cannot walk along the streets without seeing the word on every sign—National Hotel, National boot-black, National black-smith, National Oyster-house." Some in the gallery must have laughed, but Tyler was deadly serious. The states had been reduced to "mere petty corporations, provinces of one consolidated government. These principles gave to this government authority to veto all state laws, not merely by Act of Congress, but by the sword and the bayonet." Not only was nationalism "untrue and illogical," it was "anti-American." America was a compact of states and the federal government was their creature, not their sovereign. Nothing could have been farther from Jackson's conception of the Union.

He paused to look around at his colleagues, who sat in stony silence. Jackson's proclamation and the Force Bill, he continued, would "place the President at the head of the regular army in array against the States, and the sword and the cannon would come to be the common arbiter. . . . I would peril all, everything that I hold most dear, if I could be the means of stilling the agitated bellows." The Jacksonians, though, were the clear majority, and he appealed to their consciences. "If war should grow out of this measure, you are alone responsible." He refused to believe that there was not one man among them who would "step forward to rescue his country in this her moment of peril."[32]

While Tyler would act "as a sentinel upon the watch-tower to give the alarm on the approach of tyranny," he was also willing to compromise for peace. Following his speech, Senator William Cabell Rives, Tyler's fellow Virginian but a loyal Jacksonian, argued vigorously in favor of the bill and declared resistance to it "unconstitutional," a sign that Tyler's position might cost him reelection.[33] Indeed, Jacksonians in western Virginia now urged James McDowell, a popular member of the House of Delegates, to run against Tyler, and after his Senate speech some of his supporters deserted him. On February 15, McDowell was nominated along with Tyler and four other men. After the votes were counted, Tyler emerged victorious with a majority of one.[34]

Meanwhile, the nullification crisis seemed to be easing. A bill designed to reduce the tariff, supported by the administration, was under debate in Congress, so the South Carolina legislature postponed dire action. Then, on February 12, Henry Clay introduced a compromise tariff bill, which quickly won the support of John C. Calhoun.[35]

But the president was taking no chances. Hearing rumors that the Force Bill might be tabled in the Senate, he ordered his surrogates to "rush that bill thro [sic]. . . . This is due to the country, it is

due to me & to the safety of this union." He asked that every senator's vote be formally recorded so that "the nullifiers may all be distinguished from those who are in support of the laws, & and the
union." But when the Force Bill finally came to a vote on February
20, the nullifiers as well as their opponents left the chamber without voting yeah or nay. Among them were John C. Calhoun, who
was violently opposed to the measure; Henry Clay, who was
strongly in favor; and Thomas Hart Benton, a Jackson man, who
was skeptical. Virginia's other senator and Tyler's critic, William
Rives, abstained. The final tally was thirty-two in favor, one opposed. Only Tyler, who was himself not a nullifier, had the courage
to vote against. No other vote cast in his long career gave him more
pleasure: "Against that odious measure my name stands conspicu-
ously," he said later, "since it is the only vote recorded in the nega-
tive on . . . that bloody bill."[36]

Six days later, the House easily passed the Compromise Tariff
Bill of 1833, and on March 1 the Senate, with John Tyler voting
yes, approved the measure with votes to spare. The nullification
crisis was over. Perhaps more than any other Southerner, Tyler had
helped to bring about that outcome. He had encouraged Clay to
lead the effort and brought him together with Calhoun to work
out an acceptable settlement. That effort also gave him great pride.
At a banquet at the Gloucester County Courthouse, organized by
his supporters, Tyler raised his glass: "[To] Virginia, the blessed
mother of us all; he who denies her his allegiance and shall refuse
to come to her rescue in her hour of peril and her danger, is un-
worthy to be called her son."[37]

• • •

The happy interlude did not last. President Jackson, emboldened by
his victories over Clay and the nullifiers, moved to complete his destruction of the Second Bank of the United States. In September
1833, Jackson ordered the removal of federal funds from the bank,
placing them in twenty-three state depositories, called "pet banks."
Nicholas Biddle, Jackson's old foe, leaped to the battle. "This worthy

President thinks that because he has scalped Indians and imprisoned Judges he is to have his way with the Bank," he mocked. "He is mistaken." Biddle ordered the bank to call in debts, refuse to extend loans, and tighten credit, all of which damaged the economy.[38]

No man despised the bank more than Tyler, but he resisted Jackson's dictatorial tendencies. "Concede to the President the power to dispose of the public money as he pleases," he wrote Henry Curtis, "and it is vain to talk of check[s] and balances. The presidential office swallows up all power, and the president becomes every inch a king." Clay, whose political stock had risen when he held back the cries for civil war, took the opportunity to build a coalition of disaffected Jacksonians. "We are in the midst of a revolution," he told the Senate, "rapidly tending towards a total change of the pure republican character of the Government, and to the concentration of all power in the hands of one man. . . . If the Congress does not apply an instantaneous remedy, the fatal collapse will soon come." He introduced resolutions to censure Jackson, who, he charged, "has assumed upon himself authority and power not conferred by the Constitution and laws, but in derogation of both." Clay hoped his new coalition would finally win him the presidency in 1836.[39]

Virginia's citizens were suffering from the bank's new policies, so Tyler supported Clay's resolutions and urged that the federal funds be restored. "The administration is evidently sinking," he wrote Letitia on February 17, 1834, "and I do not doubt that in six months it will be almost flat. . . . I have not yet spoken, but everybody seems anxious to hear me." A week later, he told a crowded Senate chamber that he still believed the bank was unconstitutional and hoped to see it die, but Jackson's act was illegal. The president had seized powers, creating his own rich and powerful state banks. "Give the President control over the purse," he warned, "and I care not what you call him, he is 'every inch a king.'" Jackson's veto of the rechartering of the bank prevented it from dying slowly without disrupting the economy. Now his attack on the dying institution had thrown it "into convulsions." The funds must be returned. Tyler even proposed that Congress should submit the question of the bank's future to the people in the form of a constitutional amendment. Above all, "if the Bank must die, let it die by law. . . . By that I will stand."

For the first time, Tyler publicly revealed his disenchantment with Jackson's leadership of Jefferson's Democratic-Republican Party. He called Jackson's Democrats "a party which changes its principles, as the chameleon its color, with every cloud or ray which proceeds from the presidential orb." He could not belong to a party "which denounces the tariff, and yet votes for and sustains the tariff of 1828—that Bill of Abominations . . . a party which denounces the Bank and sustains the Force Bill; which denounces the Bank and even now sustains the President in his assumption of power conferred neither by the laws nor the Constitution. No, sir, I belong not to that . . . party." The country's only hope, Tyler suggested, was the new Whig Party that was forming under Henry Clay's leadership. He was not yet ready to formally join it, but he had clearly become an ally.[40]

Other Virginians were leaving the Jackson fold. Tyler's friend Littleton W. Tazewell was elected governor of the commonwealth in March 1834, and anti-Jacksonians took control of the new General Assembly. That body instructed Tyler and his Senate colleague William Rives to vote for Clay's censure resolutions. Rives would not and resigned his seat. The assembly appointed Benjamin W. Leigh, a "Tidewater grandee" of the Whig persuasion, to replace him. On March 28, Leigh, Tyler, and twenty-four other senators voted to censure Jackson. Twenty senators stood with the president, including Thomas Hart Benton, who pledged to fight forever until the censure was formally expunged from the Senate's records.[41]

Censuring the president was "an unprecedented action" that brought a strong protest from Jackson, who claimed his actions were entirely legal and constitutional and reflected the wishes expressed by the American people in his landslide victory of 1832. "The President is the direct representative of the American people," Jackson proclaimed. For those now calling themselves Whigs, this was political and philosophical heresy. Republican government, they passionately believed, rested on the idea that Congress—not the president—represented the people's will. Although the Senate rejected Jackson's protest and endorsed the censure, Tyler's worst nightmare had come true: "King Numbers" led by "King One" controlled the government.[42]

Tyler's prediction in February 1834 that Jackson's movement would soon be "flat" proved incorrect, especially in Virginia. In spring 1835, Tazewell and his supporters were routed by the Jacksonians, who again proved to be superb organizers and practitioners of a new politics of rallies, parades, and popular appeals. With control of both houses of the Virginia assembly, the Jacksonians targeted for elimination Senators John Tyler and Benjamin Leigh, two of their beloved president's staunchest critics. The instrument of their destruction would be the venerated "doctrine of instructions." In the next session of Congress, Senator Thomas Hart Benton's motion to expunge Jackson's censure, defeated on two earlier occasions, would come up and the House of Delegates would instruct Tyler and Leigh to vote for it. When the two men refused, they would be forced to resign their seats.[43]

Yet Leigh and Tyler had another option. While both men supported instruction, they had made it clear that they would not vote for measures they deemed unconstitutional. The Constitution required Congress to record proceedings in a journal; it did not provide for the actual destruction of those pages, as specified in Benton's resolution. If the measure passed, an important event in the Senate's history would be obliterated, as if it never happened. "I will not obey instructions which shall require me to vote for a gross violation of the Constitution," Leigh wrote Tyler in July 1835.[44]

Tyler was not as certain. Friends recommended that he follow Leigh's example and unite against the Jacksonians, but one Whig ally suggested that both Tyler and Leigh resign, lest they be accused of wanting to cling to power for personal gain. An anti-Jackson campaign might also destroy the Whigs' chances of defeating Vice

President Martin Van Buren in the next presidential contest. There was talk about a Vice President Tyler, and Virginia's Whigs actually nominated him. But in early February 1836, Virginia's assembly approved what Tyler called "the villainous instructions"; he could no longer delay a decision.

"My resolution is fixed, and I shall resign," he wrote his son Robert. Retirement, he had told him, held "no horror for me; for, come when it may, I have the satisfaction to know that I have been honest in the worst of times." When Clay and Calhoun learned of Tyler's decision, they tried to persuade him to stay. "Gentlemen, the first act of my political life was a censure of Messrs. Giles and Brent for opposition to instructions," Tyler explained. "The chalice presented to their lips is now presented to mine, and I will drain it even to the dregs." Calhoun seemed incredulous, then replied: "If you make it a point of personal honor, we have nothing more to say."[45]

In his formal letter of resignation, Tyler explained that he could not subscribe to such an unconstitutional resolution. If it were passed, the Senate would become "a secret conclave, where deeds the most revolting might be performed in secrecy and darkness." Honor and principles remained his only guideposts. "Parties are continually changing," he concluded. "The man of to-day gives place to the man of to-morrow, and the idols which one set worships, the next destroy. The only object of my political worship shall be the Constitution. . . . I shall carry with me into retirement the principles which I brought with me into public life, and by the surrender of the high state to which I was called by . . . the people of Virginia, I shall set an example to my children which shall teach them to regard as nothing place and office, when either is to be attained or held at the sacrifice of honor." His fellow senators must have appreciated Tyler's moral stand because, not long before Tyler retired, they elected him president pro tempore, a post then held by only the most highly regarded. His enemies in the Virginia assembly had the final word, however. To replace Tyler, they elected William C. Rives.[46]

Tyler returned to Virginia in early March 1836, a few weeks before his forty-sixth birthday. Half his life had been spent in politics, but now he looked forward to a private life. "Perhaps I am doomed to perpetual exile from the public councils," he wrote. "If so, I am content."

3

Tippecanoe and Tyler Too

Once again, John Tyler's retirement was short-lived. As a former governor, congressman, and senator, he was inevitably drawn into the developing political tempest of his day. President Jackson had "swept over the Government . . . like a tropical tornado," creating a backlash that turned the new Whig movement into a storm of equal ferocity.[1]

The Whigs were far from an organized party, more a "loose confederation of warring factions . . . bound vaguely together by a common hatred of the new popular democracy" typified by Jackson and Martin Van Buren, his successor. The party included National Republicans, who represented Northern and northeastern merchants, industrialists, and shippers; they believed in the American System of internal improvements, a national bank, and protective tariffs. Henry Clay, Daniel Webster, and John Quincy Adams were their leaders. There were also the old Jeffersonian states' rights Southerners, who had broken with Jackson over the Force Bill—and much else besides. Most were strict constructionists who felt the presidency had become too powerful, as well as the gentleman aristocrats like Tyler, who despised the word "national" and feared the common people, whom that "bloody, bawdy, lecherous villain" Jackson claimed to represent. Finally, there were the political oddities: South Carolina slaveholders and nullifiers; alienated Democrats in New York, Pennsylvania, and Ohio who hated slavery and states' rights but hated Jackson and Van Buren's machine politics more; the exotic anti-Mason party, which was opposed to the secret societies its members felt had taken over America's government.[2]

When this unstable coalition of the disaffected had faced Vice President Martin Van Buren in 1836, all had been confusion. Local leaders eventually selected three candidates, each representing different regions and interests. For New England, there was Massachusetts senator Daniel Webster. Westerners liked General William Henry Harrison, veteran of the Battle of Tippecanoe—the Whig version of Andrew Jackson. The South's favorite son was Tennessee senator Hugh Lawson White, a former Jacksonian from the president's home state. Ironically, nobody wanted the party's founder and most eloquent spokesman, Henry Clay, probably because he was a two-time loser. As if this were not crazy enough, Virginia nominated both Harrison, who appealed especially to the mountaineers of the west, and White, who was supported in the Tidewater and Piedmont regions. Yet there was method in the Whig madness. With such a crowded field, it was conceivable that no single candidate would receive a majority, throwing the election to the House of Representatives, where the Whigs' chances might be better.

To complicate things more, Whigs in Virginia, Tennessee, North Carolina, and Georgia had chosen John Tyler as their vice presidential nominee. His supporters called on him to visit "every man's house, talk to him as tho' everything was in his power—flatter the wife and daughters and praise the hogs." But Tyler believed the Whigs' strategy was hopeless, so he stayed home and waited for their defeat. Henry Clay was discouraged. The Whigs, he said, were "cut up and divided against themselves."[3]

The various Whig tickets did better than Clay and Tyler had expected. Van Buren won, but with only 50.9 percent of the popular vote, only thirty thousand more than the combined Whig total. If twelve hundred Pennsylvanians had switched their votes, Van Buren would have lacked a majority and the election would have been decided by the House, as the Whigs had wanted. Harrison won seven states, including three that Jackson carried in 1828 and in 1832—New Jersey, Ohio, and Indiana—but Van Buren had run strongly in the South. Tyler won four states and forty-seven electoral votes (in Virginia, he outscored the Whig presidential candidate), which helped to deny Van Buren's running mate, Richard Johnson of Kentucky, a majority. For the first time in history, the vice presidential election was decided in the Senate, where Johnson was elected. Whig politicians, reading these results, recognized that the best ticket for 1840 should include a general and a Southerner.[4]

. . .

Martin Van Buren had barely assumed the presidency when economic disaster struck. It was called the Panic of 1837, but "panic" does not do justice to the catastrophe that ensued. The worst depression in American history until the 1929 Wall Street crash, its causes—including Jackson's destruction of the Bank of the United States and the removal of controls over speculation and credit expansion—are less important than its consequences. Inflation skyrocketed, and with it the price of staples such as wheat, flour, and bread. In Manhattan, posters cropped up: "Bread, Meat, Rent, Fuel—Their Prices Must Come Down. The Voice of the People Shall Be Heard, and Will Prevail." Mercantile houses closed their doors. Banks failed as people rushed to withdraw their savings, crying "pay, pay," one observer noted. "Women were nearly pressed to death and the stoutest men could scarcely contain themselves." As summer approached, almost 90 percent of the East's factories had shut down. In Pennsylvania, thousands of coal miners lost their jobs. Philip Hone, former mayor of New York and a Whig activist, wrote in his diary, "Where will it all end?—In ruin, revolution, perhaps civil war?"[5]

Van Buren called Congress into special session to unveil what came to be known as the "Sub-Treasury Plan." It called for an "Independent Treasury" in Washington and special federal depositories for government revenue, which would no longer be held by state banks. It took two years to make its way through Congress before becoming law and had no impact on the deepening crisis.[6]

Van Buren's misfortune benefited the Whigs. In the 1837 off-year elections, Whigs triumphed at the polls in Maine, Rhode Island, New York, New Jersey, Pennsylvania, Indiana, Kentucky, and Tennessee. "God bless" the people, Clay cried, "God bless them forever." The following year, the economy improved slightly but dipped again as the next presidential election approached.[7]

Tyler was not thinking about another vice presidential candidacy at the time. In 1839, he was focused entirely on returning to the Senate. A victory would be doubly pleasurable because it would mean defeating the abhorred William Cabell Rives. Winning the election would not be easy. The Virginia General Assembly was split into three unequal factions. The Whigs held eighty-one seats, the Van Buren Democrats held sixty-nine, and the Conservative Democrats—those who had broken with Van Buren but were not quite ready to become Whigs—numbered sixteen. The Conservative Democrats favored Rives. Still, Tyler was hopeful as the assembly gathered to vote on February 15.[8]

Tyler led on the first ballot with sixty-two votes, but he realized immediately that he was in trouble. Rives was showing surprising strength for a man with little more than a dozen supporters. On the fourth ballot, Tyler's caucus began to fade; Democrat John Y. Mason led, with Rives in third place but coming up fast. When rumors began to circulate that Henry Clay was supporting Rives, Congressman Henry A. Wise met with Clay to uncover the machinations. It was a very "stormy" meeting: Clay, without batting an eye, admitted his support. Wise, a "fiery young man," was incredulous. How could Clay reject Tyler, who gave up his Senate seat rather than vote to expunge the censure, and favor Rives, who did? It was part of his larger strategy to win Virginia in the forthcoming presidential campaign, Clay explained, according to Wise's perhaps exaggerated account. Rives and his conservative Democrats must be lured into the Whig camp. If Tyler dropped out and asked his supporters to vote for Rives, Clay promised, "Mr. Tyler [would] be nominated on the Whig ticket for the Vice Presidency in 1840."

It appears no formal deal was struck because Tyler continued to oppose Rives, denying him a majority. After twenty-eight ballots did not produce a winner, the General Assembly adjourned indefinitely. Tyler's behavior during the whole affair was not that of a man angling for the vice presidency. His decision to block Rives cost him the support of Virginia's Whigs who, in September, refused to honor their most distinguished citizen with the vice presidential nomination. Instead, they endorsed New York senator Nathaniel P. Tallmadge, who supported Whig economic policies, which could not have pleased Tyler in the least.[9]

Yet Tyler stuck by Clay when the "Democratic Whig National Convention" met in Harrisburg, Pennsylvania, in December 1839. Clay was hopeful of winning the nomination, collecting votes throughout the country, especially in Southern states such as Virginia, Mississippi, Louisiana, Alabama, and North Carolina. But in courting Southerners, Clay had publicly attacked the abolitionist movement and alienated influential antislavery Whigs in New York and Pennsylvania. Thurlow Weed, the Whig editor of the *Albany Journal*, argued that Clay could never carry the Empire State and was thus doomed to lose; Thaddeus Stevens, the angry clubfooted lawyer and future Radical Republican, decried Clay to be "a Mason and a loser." Together they engaged in procedural shenanigans and dirty tricks until Clay's candidacy was fatally wounded. General William Henry Harrison won the nomination. When Clay heard the news, he became completely unglued. "It is a diabolical intrigue, I know now, which has betrayed me," he moaned. "I am the most unfortunate man in the history of parties, always run by my friends when sure to be defeated, and now betrayed for a nomination when I, or any one, would be sure of an election."[10]

Tyler was also greatly disappointed by Clay's defeat. Indeed, some said that he actually broke down and cried when he heard that Clay lost, although he later denied it. But the rumor may have helped his own political fortunes, according to Weed, who believed that Tyler's tears—real or imagined—"gave him the nomination for Vice President." Had Clay, the Kentucky slave owner, won, he would have sought a running mate from the North. But Harrison had settled in Ohio and looked South for his vice president, preferably a Clay man who would help him mend fences with the party's leaders. Virginia senator Benjamin Leigh was not interested in the office, and the candidacies of South Carolina's William Preston and North Carolina's Willie Magnum elicited little interest. Senator John Clayton of Delaware, a Clay stalwart, was a possibility, but he said he would not ride to power over his dear friend's body. That left John Tyler, who had appealing strengths. A Clay supporter and former governor and senator from Virginia, which had the third greatest number of electoral votes in the country, he had also made a decent showing in the 1836 election. Although Tyler later claimed that he did not seek the job, "the office went a-begging" and, according to Weed, "was given to Tyler because no one else would have it." Tyler won the nomination "by default."[11]

Tyler expressed pleasure at the prospect of serving with General Harrison, the hero of Tippecanoe. "To have my name associated with that of the eminent patriot . . . is . . . no ordinary honour," he wrote. "The friend and supporter of Jefferson, of Madison, and of Monroe, and the immediate descendent of a signer of the Declaration of Independence, can be none other than true to his early Republican creed." That the real Harrison was not quite the great man described by Tyler indicated that he was prepared to play the political game with the best of them. And, to further console the Clay men, Tyler withdrew his Senate candidacy, thus allowing William C. Rives to finally win the election.[12]

No one attending the convention seems to have given any thought to the possibility that General Harrison, at sixty-seven the oldest man ever to seek the presidency, might die in office and, therefore, should have a vice president with compatible views. Everyone knew that Tyler was often fiercely independent and that his basic philosophy differed from the Whigs. "I was . . . wholly unquestioned about my opinions," Tyler said, adding that he was "perfectly and entirely silent in that convention." Of course, silence was the Whigs' best strategy for winning the White House. The party left Harrisburg without issuing a party platform or a statement describing its principles or plans; to do so risked tearing apart the fragile Whig coalition just at the moment when victory seemed likely.[13]

. . .

At first, Democrats rejoiced at Harrison's nomination, calling the General "Granny," a candidate more ready for retirement than the White House. "Give [Harrison] a bottle of hard cider," wrote a hostile Baltimore reporter, "settle a pension of two thousand dollars a year on him, and . . . he will sit for the remainder of his days in his log cabin by the side of a sea-coal fire, studying moral philosophy." Harrison's advisors had a better feel for the American temperament in that year of depression and quickly adopted log cabins and hard cider as the symbols of their party. "The Log Cabin is a symbol of nothing that Van Burenism knows, feels, or appreciates," wrote Weed, the Whig's most skillful propagandist. "It tells of the hopes of the humble, of the privations of the poor . . . it is the emblem of rights that the vain and insolent aristocracy of federal office-holders has . . . trampled upon."

A log cabin fever soon swept the country. Newspapers contained instructions on how to build them, and log cabin raisings, complete with plenty of hard cider or "Old Cabin Whiskey" for the tired and thirsty, were celebrated like holidays. Whig entrepreneurs created a host of products to connect the people to their candidate. There was "Tippecanoe Shaving Soap or Log-Cabin Emollient"; the "Harrison and Tyler necktie"; the "beautiful pongee handkerchief," bearing a picture of "the American flag and likeness of General Harrison"; and more, much, much more.[14]

Under the skillful hands of his Whig handlers, Harrison, an upper-class Virginian by birth who lived not in a log cabin but in a sixteen-room mansion on a three-thousand-acre Ohio plantation, was transformed into "Old Tip," the Whig answer to Old Hickory. Musicians celebrated him in song:

> Let Van from his coolers of silver drink wine,
> And lounge on his cushioned settee.
> Our man on a buck-eye bench can recline,
> Content with hard cider is he,
> The iron-armed soldier, the true-hearted soldier,
>   the gallant old soldier of Tippecanoe!

President Van Buren, the son of a New York tavern owner, became "King Mat," who wore "robes of regal state," slept in a bed of "silken down with menial servants waiting round," and sipped "from a china cup with a golden spoon."[15]

The old soldier was also a better campaigner than the Whigs hoped and the Democrats expected. Initially reluctant to actually go to the people to seek their votes (it was both unseemly and just not done), his aides eventually persuaded him to hit the campaign trail. In Dayton, Ohio, on September 10, 1840, Harrison addressed an audience estimated at one hundred thousand, "the largest political rally in the half century of the republic." Harrison told the people what they came to hear. "I am a true, simple Republican," he said, "aghast that the government under 'King Mat' is now a practical monarchy!" When he became president, he would "reduce the power and influence of the National Executive," and would retire after serving only one term. The people roared their approval.[16]

Many historians have denounced the 1840 campaign, calling it "ridiculous," "preposterous," and "one of the greatest political shell games in American history." "Every weakness of the American party system was exaggerated," wrote Herbert Agar, "the tendency to choose inconspicuous and feeble candidates; the tendency to substitute songs . . . for a discussion of issues; the tendency to promise, in private, all things to all people, while avoiding in public any language that could be construed to mean anything." It was a campaign that gave full birth to the political "image makers," but the rallies, parades, and general malarkey energized millions of Americans and gave them a peaceful outlet for their frustrations.[17]

Tyler played no major role in the campaign and he found the new politics extremely distasteful. But, in the late summer, when Vice President Richard Johnson decided to campaign for reelection, the Whigs convinced Tyler to show himself to the people. Regrettably, he left his "very large and . . . pleasant home" in Williamsburg for uncomfortable travel on steamboat and stage coach to make appearances in Washington, D.C., Virginia, Ohio, and Pennsylvania. It was an exhausting trip. At a Pittsburgh convention, he spoke to a crowd so large that it was impossible to determine its actual size, somewhere between 27,000 and 60,000 people—King Numbers, indeed. He seems to have done well in this strange, new environment, despite suffering from attacks of "bilious fever" and a hoarse voice. "Governor Tyler is a fine looking man," noted the Cleveland, Ohio, *Herald*, "plain and perfectly Republican in his dress and manners." Women found him particularly attractive. "His face with its blue eyes and the now famous Tyler nose were of the Grecian model," one fan wrote, going on to say she found him a man of "incomparable sweetness." Even his Democratic critics had to admit that he was "a graceful easy speaker," before adding that he possessed "the blandness of manner which belongs to the Virginia character."[18]

His speeches hit all the right political notes. He pointed out that he and General Harrison shared a common heritage—both their fathers fought "side by side in maintaining the rights of their country in the days of the Revolution." Now, the people faced an equally serious crisis—"the oppression of domestic tyranny." With Harrison in the White House, he proclaimed, "The day of your deliverance is at hand."[19]

There were, however, bumps in the campaign road. He was heckled in Ohio and Pennsylvania by Democrats who demanded to know his current views on national banks and protective tariffs. Tyler dodged and weaved with all the skill of a modern candidate who did not want to damage his ticket. "I am in favor of what General Harrison and Mr. Clay are in favor of," he claimed. "Between General Harrison, Mr. Clay and myself, there is no difference of opinion." Tyler's most favorable biographer, Oliver P. Chitwood, thought Tyler's behavior shameful: "[T]hat he stooped to the low practices of this charlatanic campaign is a source of real regret to his admirers. [A] man of his views had no right to assume a place of leadership in a party the majority of whose members advocated measures which he had spent a life career in opposing." True, perhaps, but it also suggests that historians would make poor politicians.[20]

What proved decisive in the end was not Harrison and Tyler's obfuscations or Whig demagoguery but the simple fact that the Panic of 1837, and Van Buren's failure to end it, inspired Americans to vote decisively for change. "Farewell, dear Van," went one Whig song,

> You're not our man;
> To guide the ship
> We'll try old Tip.

Harrison won nineteen states and 234 electoral votes, with 53 percent of the popular vote, to Van Buren's six states and 60 electoral votes. Though Harrison's margin of victory was less than 150,000 votes, he triumphed in every region of the Union. Van Buren carried only one Northern state (New Hampshire); two Western states (Missouri and Illinois); and four Southern states (South Carolina, Arkansas, Alabama, and, to Tyler's great embarrassment, Virginia. "The Goths may have taken Rome," cried the *Richmond Enquirer*, "but the Citadel is saved.") The Whigs also took control of both houses of Congress and most state governorships and legislatures. Political participation had grown astronomically between 1836 and 1840: 900,000 new voters went to the polls, three-fifths of them to vote for Harrison and the Whigs.[21]

. . .

The new vice president–elect read the returns with pleasure but also concern. "There are so many jarring views to reconcile and harmonize, that the work is one of immense difficulty," he wrote to his friend Henry Wise. "Let me whisper what you already know, that the branch of the Whig Party called the Nationals is composed of difficult material to manage, they are too excessive in their notions . . . and are accustomed to look upon a course of honest compromise as a concession of . . . principle." The Democrats, though shaken by defeat, shared Tyler's view. "We may be beaten, but we will not stay beaten," the journalist Thomas Ritchie predicted. "This discordant combination of the odds and ends of all parties cannot long continue. Like the image of Nebuchadnezzar, which was made of clay and brass and various materials, a single shot must shatter it to pieces." Another issue hung over the triumphant party: would the bitter Henry Clay, master of the Whig-controlled Congress, be the real chief executive?[22]

Clay probably expected that Harrison would follow his lead since Clay was primarily responsible for launching the general's career. Harrison had first come to Clay's attention when the general defeated the Shawnee Indians at the Battle of Tippecanoe, and he had watched with interest Harrison's progress during the War of 1812, urging President Madison to make use of the general's talents. A dozen years later, when he was secretary of state, Clay recommended to President Adams that Harrison become the new minister to the Court of St. James (the post went to another man). A few years later, again at Clay's urging, Harrison was appointed minister to Colombia. Clay's protégé was now the president, and no doubt Clay recalled what several of Harrison's supporters had told him: if Harrison was elected, "Mr. Clay will be the actual president of the U[nited] States."[23]

Harrison had little time to savor his victory before Clay made his first moves. During several meetings prior to the inauguration, Clay urged the appointment of his favorites to the cabinet and outlined those policies he believed Harrison should follow—the creation of a new Bank of the United States; adherence to the Compromise Tariff of 1832; and the passage of a land bill to provide funds for internal improvements. Clay also wanted to turn the president into a glorified clerk by denying him the right to seek a second term; curtailing his ability to veto bills, make appointments, and remove officials; and placing the Treasury under Congress's firm control. The new president, Clay said, should start his term by calling Congress into special session. Harrison listened politely but rejected several of Clay's preferred cabinet members in favor of his own men.

Meanwhile, Tyler, like most vice presidents, was fading into the political background. He asked Henry Wise to book him a room starting in January either at Brown's Hotel or at Mrs. McDonald's Boarding House, where he lived while in the Senate. He did not participate in the formation of the cabinet, nor did Harrison consult him about policies. But Tyler did express his views to his friends. He hoped that Harrison would be "firm and decisive to one and all," he wrote Wise. "Every eye should be kept fixed upon the official duty assigned, and never once lifted up to gaze at the succession." He was concerned that Daniel Webster's appointment as secretary of state would touch off a factional struggle, "excite the jealousy of the others and produce discontent and final rupture." Webster was not his first choice but, he added, "I can do no more than suggest." He declined to tell Wise that nobody was asking him for suggestions.[24]

By January, Harrison and Clay were openly fighting each other. When Clay complained about Harrison's choice for the powerful post of the collector of the port of New York, Harrison said, "Mr. Clay, you forget that I am President."[25]

On March 13, 1841, eight days after Harrison's inauguration, the two men argued again about the president's failure to call the special session. To nudge Harrison, Clay drafted a statement for him. Harrison exploded. Instead of asking for a personal meeting, he replied to Clay by letter. "You are too impetuous," Harrison wrote. "Much as I rely upon your judgment there are others whom I must consult & in many cases to determine adversely to your suggestions." For Clay, who thought he was dining at the White House that evening, Harrison's response "was the most humiliating rebuke of his life." A friend found the senator pacing his room, hand wrapped around Harrison's note, crushing it. "And it has come to this!" Clay yelled. "I am civilly but virtually requested not to . . . see the president personally but hereafter only communicate with him in writing."

Clay was now firmly convinced that his enemies, led by Secretary of State Daniel Webster, controlled Harrison and the government. He quickly replied, telling Harrison that he was "mortified" by the president's apparent belief that Clay was trying to act as a dictator. He denied this strongly and, in closing, told Harrison not "to trouble" himself by replying. Clay then left Washington for Kentucky, "breathing out rage and threatening all the way."

A few days later, Harrison confronted Whig partisans who were demanding that all Democratic officeholders be fired. Indiana congressman George H. Proffit described what happened next: "General Harrison . . . with a warmth and energy he rarely exhibited . . . extended his arms, exclaiming . . . , 'So help me God, I will resign my office before I can be guilty of such an iniquity.' " This drove the others from the room, but Proffit remained to hear the president say, "The Federal portion of the Whig party are making desperate efforts to seize the reins of government. They are urging the most unmerciful prescription, and if they continue to do so much longer, they will drive me mad!"[26]

On March 17, Harrison announced that Congress would meet in special session beginning on May 31. He did not use Clay's draft; the words, like the decision, were his own. It was his last major act as president. Less than three weeks later he died. John Tyler was "called from my farm to undertake the administration of public affairs," he later noted. "I foresaw that I was called to a bed of thorns."

4

Amid Earthquake and Tornado

On April 7, 1841, the political squabbling that may have hastened William Henry Harrison to his death paused momentarily while the nation buried the president. Harrison's body lay in state in the East Room of the White House, his coffin "covered with a black velvet pall," partially open so passersby could catch a final glimpse of the general. John Johnston, who had known Harrison when he was governor of the Indiana territory, thought the late president looked "calm and natural; his white hair lying close to his head, and his features regular and peaceful." In the air was a "frail scent" from the flowers that filled the room. In attendance were the new president, "visibly affected"; the Harrison cabinet; the diplomatic corps "in gorgeous dress with stars, epaulettes, gold and silver lace"; seventy-three-year-old former president and now congressman John Quincy Adams; and nearby, many members of the House and Senate.

At 11:30 a.m., the Reverend William Hawley, the rector of St. John's Church, conducted the Episcopal ceremony, reading from a Bible and prayer book that Harrison had recently purchased. Adams, the "aged misanthrope" who was usually critical of most human endeavors, thought the "ceremony was performed in a decent and unostentatious manner, with proper religious solemnity and with the simplicity congenial to our republican institutions."[1]

At noon, the coffin, carried by twenty-four pallbearers wearing white sashes, was taken outside and placed on "a magnificent funeral car drawn by eight white horses." The cortege moved slowly through the streets of Washington, Harrison's car in the lead, followed by President Tyler riding in a carriage, then by the other dignitaries. Old Whitey, the late president's favorite horse and the one he rode to his inauguration a month earlier, came last, stirrups up and riderless. The procession "was the largest ever witnessed in this city. It extended more than two miles in length, and is supposed to have contained ten thousand persons"; another estimate placed it as high as forty thousand. Bells tolled and "deep mouthed cannons" fired sixty-eight shots, one for each year of Harrison's life. Internment was at the Congressional Burying Grounds, located east of the Capitol. (A few months later, Harrison's body was removed for burial at his Ohio plantation.) President Tyler declared Friday, May 14, as a day for national mourning. And so another precedent was established—the presidential funeral, whose features were generally followed for the next 160 years.[2]

On April 9, two days after Harrison's funeral, the new president issued what some called an "inaugural address," although Tyler never described it as such. He realized that it was necessary to inform the country of his "principles." He had not conferred with Harrison prior to his death and the suddenness of events deprived Tyler of the views of his closest friends. Therefore, he decided "to follow the light of my own judgment and the prompting of my own feelings." "President Tyler's Address," as it was called by the press, was brief and vague. Addressed to his "fellow citizens," he first expressed his great regret over the death of President Harrison, an occurrence that "subjected the wisdom and sufficiency of our institutions to a new test." Never before had the office of the presidency, because of an "unforeseen contingency," "devolved" upon the vice president, but that is what the Constitution required. As president, he would "carry out the principles of that Constitution which I have sworn 'to protect, preserve, and defend.'" By explicitly stating that he had inherited the office, Tyler undercut those who believed that he was only the "acting" president. Although a few legislators raised questions about Tyler's legitimacy, both the House and the Senate later formally recognized his lawful right to the office.

Specifically, Tyler promised a foreign policy that would do justice to all nations "while submitting to injustice from none." He urged the creation of a stronger, more efficient army and navy to ensure that "the honor of the country sustain no blemish." His remarks reflected concern over recent tensions between Britain and the United States. He would also recommend policies to deal with the spoils system. As for fiscal programs, Congress would formulate them, but he alone would determine if they were constitutional. In concluding, he promised to work "to preserve unimpaired the free institutions under which we live," relying on "the intelligence and patriotism of the people," as well as "an ever-watchful and overruling Providence."[3]

The president's address and orderly transfer of power—the first following the death of a president—won Tyler praise in the Whig press and reassured the country that all would be well. "President Tyler is a Whig—a true Whig," observed the *National Intelligencer*, "and we risk nothing in expressing our entire confidence that he will fulfill in all their extent, the expectations of the People." Thurlow Weed noted that "the President's message reflects the opinions of his predecessor upon the leading opinions affecting public welfare, and has been well received by Whig members of Congress and Whig journals." More important is that Tyler succeeded in avoiding a divisive debate over his assumption of the presidency; most of the national press agreed that it was necessary, legitimate, and constitutional.[4]

· · ·

Henry Clay, recovering from an illness at his Kentucky estate, watched the events with intense interest. Harrison's death did not surprise him, given what he had seen of the general's "habits and excitement." He believed that his twenty-year relationship with

Tyler was "amicable," but he had no clear idea "what his course would be." Tyler's address reassured him that the new president would "concur in the leading measures of the Whigs," and by the end of April he wrote John Quincy Adams that he had "confident hopes of President Tyler." Tyler's presidency would be an interregnum, his government a "caretaker," until Clay could lead the Whig ticket in 1844. Tyler, Clay believed, would not stand in his way.[5]

But in early May, Tyler made it clear in a letter to Clay that he would not be Clay's "pliant tool," as many Whigs expected. While he shared the goal of ridding the country of Van Buren's Independent Treasury, Tyler was not ready to support Clay's most desired object—the creation of a new national bank. "As to a Bank, I design to be perfectly frank with you," Tyler wrote. "I would not have it urged prematurely, the public mind is still in a state of great disquietude [about] it." Furthermore, a bank that resembled Biddle's would be divisive; if it passed Congress by a close vote, businessmen would be afraid to invest in it. When the bank's charter had expired in 1836, Biddle had opened a small but self-important bank in Philadelphia, but it had recently failed. The best course, Tyler believed, was to cancel the special session due to begin at the end of the month. If Clay could not be persuaded to delay, he would need to develop a system that would meet Tyler's constitutional test.[6]

While Tyler waited for Clay's next move, he relocated his family to the White House. The Tyler family was large—by 1841, his wife, Letitia, had given birth to eight children, born with great frequency between 1815 and 1830. By the time Tyler became president, one had died and two had married and were living with their spouses. Accompanying him to the White House were two daughters (Elizabeth, eighteen, and Alice, fourteen), three sons (Robert, twenty-five, and his wife, Priscilla; John Jr., twenty-one, who acted as his father's personal secretary; and Tazewell, eleven), as well as several of Tyler's Virginia slaves, including his personal valet, Armistead.

Tyler was extremely close to his family. "My children are my principal treasures," he wrote his eldest daughter, Mary, and he did everything he could to help them lead fruitful lives. There were tutors to educate them, extra money to pay for social events, and even appointments to posts within his administration. Not long after becoming president, Tyler called his children together for a lecture on White House family values. "My children," he began, "by a deplored event I am unexpectedly elevated to the Presidency of the United States. You, as my children, of course, rise with me. . . . [T]his promotion is only temporary and if, at any moment, you should forget to sustain it with humility and meekness, the error of such a moment will be visited upon you bitterly. . . . True nobleness in soul is only evinced in never suffering station to tempt us into a forgetfulness of ourselves and of what we owe to others."[7]

Like many well-meaning parents he was not always successful in his efforts on his children's behalf. Two had troubled marriages that ended badly. One son-in-law was so abusive that Tyler appointed him a naval purser and sent him off to sea. Another in-law was placed on the government payroll to ease the financial strain on the president. John Jr. was a troubled young man who envied his brother Robert, who he thought (correctly) was his father's favorite. Forgetting the family warning about being "tempted" by their "station," John Jr. "became so distended with his dignity," observed John Quincy Adams, that he had his "visiting cards" engraved to read: "John Tyler, Jr., Private and Confidential Secretary of his Excellency John Tyler, President of the United States." Adams, annoyed by Tyler's demeanor, called young John the "upstart prince." John Jr. began to drink heavily, and his work for the president became so bad that his father eventually fired him.[8]

Most troubling, though, was his wife's declining health. In 1839, when Letitia was forty-nine years old, she suffered a serious stroke, which left her an "invalid." She spent her White House years mostly alone, sitting in a wheelchair in a second-floor bedroom, quietly knitting or reading the Bible. Although she "modestly shrank from all notoriety and evaded the public eye as much as possible," she wanted her family to lead a normal life. "Because I am ill is no reason why the young people should not enjoy themselves," she noted.

She did not participate in any White House functions except one—in 1842, she left her room briefly to observe her daughter Elizabeth's wedding.[9]

The role of First Lady fell to twenty-five-year-old Priscilla Cooper Tyler, Robert's wife and an extremely attractive former actress. Priscilla organized and hosted the many presidential social events required: twice-weekly dinners for congressmen; lavish yearly observances on New Year's Day and the Fourth of July; parties for members of the cabinet and visiting dignitaries; formal state dinners for foreign officials (who could number in the hundreds); a "grand public levee" held once a month and assorted "balls." The economy-minded Congress refused to assist the president in paying for these many events, as well as normal household needs such as light and heat. Tyler paid the bills out of his annual salary of $25,000.

For advice on how to discharge her new responsibilities, Priscilla relied on Washington's grande dame, Dolley Madison, still lively at seventy-three, "a jolly, buxom woman who dipped snuff and rouged her face like a Paris streetwalker." Dolley knew where to buy the best "spirits and wine," which White House cook could be trusted to prepare the most delicious meal, and how to handle conversation with Secretary of State Daniel Webster.

The first grand event of the Tyler years—a formal dinner for the cabinet in May 1841—was a disaster. Everything seemed to be going well when Priscilla, exhausted after a long day of preparations and caring for a sick toddler, suddenly became "deathly pale" and fainted into Webster's arms. Her husband grabbed a pitcher of ice water and doused them both. "I have disgraced myself with Father forever," Priscilla wrote. "I had to be taken to my room, and poor Mr. Webster had to be shaken off, dried and brushed, before he could resume his place at the table." The president forgave her, and Webster, having fallen under her spell, became Priscilla's best friend in the cabinet. (Later White House events fared better.)[10]

It would have been easy for any new president, even one with Tyler's aristocratic background, to be seduced by the monarchical trappings of the office. But Tyler insisted on remaining just "Plain John." One visitor to the White House was "astonished at the informality of the President in his home life." His personal schedule was little changed from his days as a lawyer, congressman, or senator. He awoke at dawn and worked at his desk. Foreign affairs came first, then responses to congressional queries and personal petitions, followed by "matters of general concern." At nine o'clock, he had breakfast with his family. Afterward, he returned to his office, where he remained until supper was served at three thirty. In the later afternoon, he saw visitors until the evening's social events. His day ended at ten o'clock. "Such is the life led by an American President," Tyler told his friend Robert McCandlish. "What say you? Would you exchange the peace and quiet of your homestead for such an office?"[11]

• • •

Tyler's presidential honeymoon ended in mid-May when Henry Clay returned to Washington to prepare for Congress's special session. Prior to leaving Kentucky, he wrote a Virginia judge: "I repair to my post in the Senate with great hopes, not however unmixed with fears. If the Executive will cordially cooperate in carrying out the Whig measures, all will be well, otherwise every thing is at hazard." But soon after Clay's arrival in the capital, the two men met and Tyler again asked him to postpone consideration of a new national bank. Clay refused. Tyler, usually the most mild-mannered of men, lost his temper. "Then, sir," he yelled, "I wish you to understand this—that you and I were born in the same district; that we have fed upon the same food, and have breathed the same natal air. Go you now then, Mr. Clay, to your end of the avenue, where stands the Capitol, and there perform your duty to the country as you shall think proper. So help me God, I shall do mine at this end of it as I think proper."

Clay was ready, indeed eager, to fight. He was sixty-four years old and may have believed that his time was running out. He "hungered" for the presidency and would not let an accident of history rob him of the office he richly deserved. Still suffering from his 1840 rejection by the Whigs, he often moaned, "Was ever man before treated as I have been & am now." To his colleagues, he seemed unusually "irascible and volatile." "He is much more imperious and arrogant with his friends than I have ever known him," New York senator Silas Wright told former president Van Buren, "and that you know, is saying a great deal." When one senator, who had talked with the president, tried to persuade Clay to back off on the bank, Clay flew into a rage and screamed: "Tyler dares not resist. I will drive him before me."[12]

Clay wanted no less than the enactment of the entire American System: new tariffs to raise needed revenue; elimination of Van Buren's sub-treasury system; a public lands bill; and, of course, creation of a third Bank of the United States. He felt confident that he had the votes; he controlled the Senate (and appointed himself chairman of the finance committee) and fellow Whigs ran the House. Said one angry Democrat, "Mr. Clay is carrying everything by storm; his will is the law of Congress." Clay, emboldened after the bill to repeal the sub-treasury system sailed through both chambers and Tyler signed it, asked Treasury Secretary Thomas Ewing for the administration's proposal for a bank charter. On June 12, Ewing sent a draft to Clay. It clearly reflected Tyler's views: the new "Fiscal Bank of the United States" would be chartered in the District of Columbia—the Constitution specifically gave Congress that right—with branches only in states that gave their approval. Clay laughed: "What a Bank that would be." The country needed a real national bank, he believed, and had endorsed one when they elected Harrison and the Whigs—not this "rickety, imbecile, incompetent local bank."

Ignoring the president, the "bold and reckless Clay" decided to create his own bank. On June 21, he proposed to the Senate a bank whose branches did not require the states' consent, which he knew Tyler would never accept. Congressman Henry Wise, Tyler's friend in the House, thought Clay wanted "to drive Tyler to a veto," then play his old role as the "Great Compromiser" by rushing in to save the nation from turmoil. During the next six days, both parties looked for a way out of this morass. On July 27, Clay presented a final version of the charter, one that bent a bit but mostly contained everything he wanted. He permitted a state to reject a branch if its state legislature passed a law doing so at its session following the enactment of the bank. But he also added an amendment that would allow the bank to create a branch over the opposition of a state whenever the bank deemed it "necessary and proper." The bill narrowly passed the Senate and won House approval on August 6. Then it was sent to the president.

Clay felt that Tyler's destruction was inevitable. A veto would likely cause the cabinet to resign, and the little support Tyler had gained among the Whigs would disappear. If he signed the bill, it would alienate Democrats and reinforce Clay's dominant role.

Rumors abounded. Days passed without word from the White House. "There is a most agonizing state of uncertainty in the public mind," Clay observed, as he and the Whigs waited. The *New York Herald* reported: "Politicians discuss it morning noon and night—in the Avenue, in the House, over their lunch . . . their coffee, their wine." John Tyler Jr. was said to have remarked, "[T]o suppose that my father can be gulled by such a humbug compromise as this bill contains is to suppose that he is an ass." Democrats hoped for a veto "that would embarrass . . . Mr. Clay," and urged it on the president. Whig congressman John Minor Botts reportedly told Tyler: "[I]f you can reconcile this bill to yourself, all is sunshine and calm: your administration will be met with the warm, hearty zealous support of the whole Whig party, and when you retire from the great theatre of National politics, it will be with the thanks, and plaudits, and approbation of your countrymen." Some heard that the president had not yet made up his mind. He planned to attend church that Sunday—August 15— and "pray earnestly and devoutly to be enlightened as to his duty."[13]

In fact, Tyler had already decided that he must veto the bill. Not only did he consider forced branching unconstitutional, the debate had shifted from what was best fiscally for the country to a personal duel for power between the president and Clay. "My back is to the wall," Tyler wrote his friend Beverley Tucker, "and while I deplore the assaults, I shall . . . beat back the assailants." To another, he explained: "I am placed upon trial. Those who have all along opposed me will still call out for further trials, and thus leave me impotent and powerless." It was now a question of honor.[14]

The next morning, August 16, John Jr. forced his way through the crowd blocking the Senate's entrance and delivered the president's message to the clerk. Regular business halted, the chamber fell silent, and the clerk began to read. As the tenor of the message became clear, visitors in the gallery hissed and booed. Missouri senator Thomas Hart Benton, no friend of Tyler's, asked that these "bank ruffians" and "hooligans" be removed, and one man was arrested. (John Quincy Adams was amused. "T. H. Benton made a ridiculous scene, till a man was taken into custody, and the doughty knight of the stuffed cravat abated his manly wrath," he wrote in his diary.) Democrats cheered the veto. "Egad," said one, "Tyler has found one of old Jackson's pens and it wouldn't write any way but plain and straight forward." Two nights later, a group of Democrats assembled at the White House to thank the president for his "patriotic and courageous" decision.[15]

Tyler's argument was consistent with his long-held belief that the bank was unconstitutional. Having taken the oath "to preserve, protect and defend" that sacred document, he had no other choice but a veto. He considered the bill's provision regarding state legislative approval hopelessly confusing. What if a state's legislature approved but not its senate? This bill was fatally flawed and he would not "sanction it."

Whig newspapers denounced the president and activists, including Philip Hone (who upon meeting Tyler thought he was "a fine, good-hearted gentleman [and] disinterested patriot"), were profoundly disappointed. Hone dubbed Tyler "Monsieur Veto" and his message "the quintessence of twaddle." Tyler had betrayed the Whigs and the dead president. "Poor Tippecanoe! It was an evil hour that

'Tyler too' was added to make out the line. There was rhyme, but no reason in it."[16]

Some unhappy Whigs decided to express their displeasure in more violent ways. At 2:00 a.m. on the morning of August 18, a drunken mob gathered outside the White House portico. They blew horns, beat drums, threw rocks at the building, and fired guns into the night sky. Tyler and his family were awakened by the noise and could hear voices crying, "A Bank! A Bank! Down with the Veto" and "Huzza for Clay!" Someone in the mansion's upstairs quarters lit candles and the light scared the crowd off. Another group arrived a few hours later, dragging a scarecrow-like figure. They set it afire and John Tyler was burned in effigy. It was "the most violent demonstration ever to occur at the White House complex." The men were later caught and brought to trial, but Tyler interceded, excusing them for their extreme political passion, which, he believed, should not be prosecuted in a free society: they were released without penalty.[17]

Clay thought the whole affair quite humorous, claiming that the ruffians were not Whigs but actually the Democrats who had visited the president with congratulations. "I think I can now see the principal dramatis personae," he said. "There stood the distinguished Senator from South Carolina [John C. Calhoun] . . . tall, careworn, with furrowed brow . . . muttering to himself . . . 'This is indeed a real crisis!' . . . Not far off the Honorable senators from Arkansas and Missouri, the latter looking at the Senator from South Carolina, with an indignant curl on his lips and scorn in his eye." Clay never missed a chance to embarrass James Buchanan of Pennsylvania, whose high-pitched voice Clay often imitated, as he did on this day. Whigs laughed and applauded his performance.[18]

Tyler was not pleased. Concerned for the welfare of his family and particularly that of his ailing wife, he asked Congress to establish a White House police force. While Congress debated the issue—some opposed the creation of a so-called palace guard—a drunken painter threw rocks at the president as he walked along the south grounds. On another occasion, a strange package arrived at the White House. Tyler, fearing it might contain a bomb, asked a guard to examine it. But when he opened the box all he found was a cake.[19]

• • •

Although Tyler "could profess high principles to the point of absurdity," he could also be surprisingly flexible. Four months after the veto, some Whigs approached him to see if a deal might be possible, and Tyler, still hoping that he might have the party's support (if not Clay's), agreed to join them in the effort. The cabinet developed yet another version of the bill, calling the institution a "fiscal corporation" rather than a "bank," which Tyler found acceptable. To Virginia congressman Alexander H. H. Stuart, he said: "If you can be instrumental in passing this bill through Congress, I will esteem you the best friend I have on earth."[20]

Just when it seemed as though the political fallout was settling, everything again came apart. On August 18, Clay finally replied on the floor of the Senate to Tyler's veto message, which he called "harsh, if not reproachful." For ninety minutes he attacked the president, although he knew that a new version of the bill would be introduced shortly in the House. Clay argued that Congress, in passing the bill, spoke for the people, and Tyler's action ignored their voices. If Tyler's principles were at risk, then he should have followed the example he set in 1836 and resigned his office. When Virginia's Senator Rives—now a Tyler ally—rose to defend the president, Clay ridiculed him. He accused Rives of wanting to create a new party for a president who was now "solitary and alone, shivering by the pitiless storm." Tyler's supporters, Clay mocked, were such a small, pathetic group that they did not even amount to a "decent corporal's guard." Clay then urged the Senate to override the president's veto. He failed to get the required two-thirds vote. (Later, he recommended a constitutional amendment that, if ratified, would have reduced the number needed to override a veto to a simple majority.)[21]

Tyler was stung by Clay's remarks but enraged when Congressman John Minor Botts, once a good friend, allowed the distribution of a letter severely critical of the president. The so-called Coffeehouse Letter, written just before the veto, accused "our Captain Tyler" of becoming the prisoner of "ambitious and designing mischief makers" in the Democratic Party. In betraying the Whigs, Tyler was now "an object of execration." Botts followed this with a blistering attack on the House floor in which he claimed that Tyler had assured him repeatedly—more than twenty times, Botts said— that a national bank was "not only necessary but indispensable, that the country could never get along without one." Thus Tyler was branded a liar and a dishonorable man.

These continuing assaults, it is believed, led Tyler to his decision to veto the second bank bill, which had undergone changes in Congress since his draft. By early September, he concluded that if he had any political future at all, it was not with the Whigs. Perhaps his future lay with the Democrats or in building a new party of both Whigs and Democrats. When the cabinet, realizing Tyler's change of heart, begged Clay to postpone a vote on a charter for the new fiscal corporation, Clay cried: "Never, never! Not if we stay here til Christmas." The bill passed overwhelmingly in the House but the Senate approved it by only five votes.[22]

Tyler's second veto message arrived on September 9. He raised the same questions about constitutionality but then explicitly extolled the instrument of the veto itself. He called it "the great conservative principle of our system," given to the president to protect the American people against the tyranny of a congressional majority. Ironically, his argument echoed Jackson's theory of presidential power, which Tyler had once heartily rejected.[23]

The veto caused a political explosion greater than the first. For years, Whig papers produced a steady stream of venom. "If a Goddirected thunderbolt were to strike and annihilate the traitor," the *Lexington Intelligencer* wrote, "all would say that 'Heaven is just.'" Tyler was called "His Accidency"; the "Executive Ass"; "base, selfish, and perfidious"; "a vast nightmare over the republic." One writer claimed that the president was insane, the victim of "brain fever."

Another, borrowing from Shakespeare, called "for a whip in every honest hand, to lash the rascal naked through the world." There were anti-Tyler rallies and demonstrations everywhere and numerous burnings in effigy, including in Richmond and at the Charles City County courthouse, where the young John Tyler had practiced law. Angry letters poured into the White House; many proffered threats on the president's life.[24]

What happened next was also expected, but it was still shocking because it had never before happened in American history: the president's entire cabinet, save Daniel Webster, resigned. It was so well choreographed that many believed Clay had designed the exodus. And it could hardly have been a coincidence that navy secretary George Badger had held a special dinner for the members of the cabinet on the evening of Tyler's veto. Webster quickly sensed the purpose of the event when he noticed a guest who was not in the president's cabinet—Senator Henry Clay—and chose to leave. After dinner, when the men gathered to discuss resignation, Clay removed himself, leaving the conspirators to arrange the day's events.[25]

Between 12:30 p.m. and 5:30 p.m. on Saturday, September 11, five members of the Whig cabinet trooped through the president's office and handed him letters of resignation. John Tyler Jr. stood beside his father's desk, armed with a watch, which he used to methodically record the time each letter was delivered. Clay hoped that prolonging the process would prevent Tyler from forming a new cabinet before the special session of Congress adjourned that Monday. Tyler would be so rattled, Clay thought, that he would resign the presidency that very night, elevating the Senate's president pro tempore, a Clay man, to the office. Or perhaps a special election might be held, which would finally bring Clay to the White House. It was a clever scheme.

At the end of the day, only Webster remained in the cabinet. The secretary of state was so torn by uncertainty and his own ambition to be president that he was an insomniac. If he left the administration, he would acknowledge Clay's control of the party. If he

stayed, he would anger Whigs without winning friends among conservative Democrats. He was also then involved in delicate diplomatic negotiations with the British, which he wanted to complete.
Webster met with the president. "Where am I to go, Mr. President?" Webster asked.

"You must decide that for yourself, Mr. Webster," Tyler replied.

"If you leave it to me, Mr. President," Webster said, "I will stay
where I am."

Tyler rose and said: "Give me your hand on that, and now I will
say to you that Henry Clay is a doomed man from this hour." The
two men shook hands, united only in their hatred of the senator.[26]

Clay was outfoxed, if not doomed. It was not the first time Clay
mistook Tyler's "affability for malleability." He would not leave the
presidency because Clay hatched a ploy. "My resignation would
amount to a declaration to the world that our system of government has failed," Tyler noted. "[T]hat the provision made for the
death of the President was . . . so defective as to merge all executive powers in the legislative branch of the government. . . . The
light reflected from burning effigies served to render the path of
duty more plain." Tyler had suspected for some time that this moment was coming and had already selected a new cabinet. The new
attorney general, Hugh S. Legaré, and navy secretary, Abel P. Upshur, shared Tyler's commitment to states' rights. But the remaining members—the new secretary of war, John C. Spencer, secretary
of the Treasury, Walter Forward, and postmaster general, Charles
Wickliffe—were all Whigs with independent state backing; they
also all supported the party's congressional program but disliked
Clay. Wickliffe, in particular, was "Clay's most bitter personal enemy" in his own state of Kentucky. Furthermore, the Tyler cabinet
was equally balanced between North and South.[27]

With these appointments, Tyler was sending a signal that he was
not, as some charged, a prisoner of a "Virginia cabal" or "corporal's
guard" and, more important, that he was still willing to work with
those Whigs who were not Clay's vassals. Indeed, during the next
few months, Tyler even built a shaky relationship with influential

Whigs Thurlow Weed and Horace Greeley, as well as staunch anti-Clay figures. His efforts "split the Whig leadership" and weakened Clay's position. Of all the observers who tried to analyze Tyler, John C. Calhoun may have come closest. "[He] is essentially a man for the middle ground," he noted during that "tempest tossed" first year, and "he will attempt to take a middle position now." Calhoun may have also been correct in stating that, in those early days, there had been no middle ground.[28]

Tyler's appointments were submitted to the special session of the Senate on Monday, September 13, and were immediately approved. After Congress adjourned, a group of Whigs, numbering between fifty and eighty, gathered at "Capitol Square" to approve a declaration of principles and to inform the American people of their plans. Tyler was, of course, the chief recipient of their wrath, the symbol of the kind of despotic president they vowed to destroy. To prevent a continuation of the "suffering" experienced under Jackson and Tyler, future presidents would be allowed to serve no more than one term; their powers of appointment and removal would be severely restricted—for instance, the secretary of the Treasury would be chosen by and be responsible to Congress; and a constitutional amendment limiting veto power would be submitted to the states. At the conclusion of their ceremony, the Whigs formally expelled Tyler from their party. Never in American history had a president been ejected from the party that had brought him to power.[29]

. . .

Later that night, an exultant Henry Clay told his supporters that Tyler was "a President without a party." The speech was vintage Clay—melodramatic, patriotic, and maudlin. "This is a dark night," he proclaimed. "There is no moon, and the little stars are slumbering in their beds, behind the dark canopy that is spread over the heavens." But they should not despair. They had fought the good fight against a president he now called a traitor: "[B]enedict Arnold escaped to England after his treason was detected. . . . Tyler is on his way to the Democratic camp. They may give him lodgings in some outhouse, but they never will trust him. He will stand here, like Arnold in England, a monument of his perfidy and disgrace."[30]

Who bore the major responsibility for this political deadlock? While Clay, in the view of historian Robert Remini, tried to force "the President and the Whig party into accepting what he, and he alone, had decided the American people had mandated in the election of 1840," Tyler could be criticized for being "weak minded, muddled, and vacillating." Clay was definitely a narcissist, obsessed with getting his own way, and Tyler often seemed confused as to which party he should join. The answer, though, lies in the complex political environment in which Tyler was forced to operate. As a former vice president without a strong national political base, he was trapped between the Democrats, who thought him a turncoat, and the Whigs, led by a man who sought to replace him, sooner rather than later. The storm and stress of the special session obscured the Whig legislation Tyler signed into law: the repeal of the sub-treasury, aid to the nation's debtors, and a land bill giving squatters the right to acquire land cheaply. Equally important was Tyler's defense of presidential prerogatives. Had Harrison lived, the presidency, as Tyler later noted, might well have been seriously weakened. "So far . . . [my] administration has been conducted amid earthquake and tornado," Tyler observed. "I think that it should be fairly entitled to some small share of praise as to set off the torrents of abuse."[31]

5

Abused as Never Before

On September 13, 1841, Congress entered recess and Tyler enjoyed a brief respite from the partisan warfare. In October, he left Washington for the first time since April for a trip combining business and pleasure in Virginia. He examined military fortifications and naval installations in Norfolk and Hampton Roads, then moved on to Williamsburg, where he was welcomed by his friends. When he stopped briefly in Richmond, the cool displeasure of the city's Whigs was evident.[1]

Tyler hoped that a negotiated approach might win him support: "moderation," he once noted, "is the mother of true wisdom." Unfortunately, as John C. Calhoun feared, the middle ground had fully disappeared. Bank closures and farm bankruptcies led to stunning Whig defeats in the fall 1841 elections, and Democrats took control of governorships and state legislatures from Maine to Mississippi. The "relief and reform" promised by the Whigs in 1840 had not occurred and voters blamed the party. But Henry Clay had another explanation for the electoral catastrophe. "An army which believes itself betrayed by its commander-in-chief, will never fight well under him," he asserted. Afraid that the Whigs were threatened with extinction, activists decided to back Clay even more intensely. This meant renewing the struggle with Tyler when

Congress convened in December. It was "war to the knife," in historian Michael Holt's words.[2]

For Tyler, Washington was again a bed of thorns. In his December message to Congress, Tyler proposed the creation of yet another new banking system, which he called the "Exchequer Plan," an unstable combination of Whig, Democratic, and Tyler economic principles. One hostile paper called it "a ridiculous imbecility," another "a dangerous grant, that might subvert the Constitution." Clay rejected it as the fantasies of "a poor, deluded man," and tabled it without debate or a final decision. These struggles with the president exhausted Clay, so he resigned his Senate seat to rest and to prepare for the 1844 presidential campaign.[3]

With the country on the brink of financial collapse and the Compromise Tariff of 1833 due to expire in June 1842, the tariff debate again became bitter. Clay's surrogates wanted a tariff increase, with protection for specific industries and distribution of funds from land sales. Tyler would not accept distribution or protection, but grudgingly agreed to support a higher tariff that could provide needed revenue. After months of haggling, Congress sent Tyler a bill heavy with Clay's handiwork. The president vetoed it. So frequent and regular were Tyler's vetoes that this one was called "his veto of the month." By now the Whig strategy was clear: produce legislation that the president could not support. "The more Vetoes the better," Clay chortled. "The inevitable tendency of events is to impeachment." For Tyler, the battle was no joke. Clay and the Whigs were a threat to the Union. Tyler's navy secretary spoke the president's mind when he wrote to a friend: "I should not be surprised to hear of popular outbreaks in all the large cities, and of desperate measures calculated to overthrow all law and order."[4]

On July 10, following the veto of the latest tariff bill, Congressman John Minor Botts, author of the Coffeehouse Letter that had politically wounded Tyler, introduced a resolution that would create a special committee to investigate whether the president should be impeached, the first time such an inquiry had been called. The

resolution was approved and thirteen committee members selected. Tyler enemy John Quincy Adams was elected chairman.
When the news reached the president, he was stunned. To his
friend Robert McCandlish, Tyler explained, "Did you ever expect
to see your old friend under trial for 'high crimes and misde-
meanors?' " he wrote. "The high crime of sustaining the Constitution of the country I have committed, and I plead guilty. The high
crime of . . . daring to have an opinion of my own, Congress to the
contrary not withstanding, I plead guilty also to that; and if these
be impeachable matters, why then I ought to be impeached. . . . I
am abused, in Congress and out, as a man never was before—
assailed as a traitor, and threatened with impeachment. But let it
pass. Other attempts are to be made to head me, and we shall see
how they succeed."[5]

Tyler did not receive a fair hearing from Adams's committee. Its
final report, released on August 16, 1842, concluded that Tyler had
committed "offenses of the gravest character" and deserved to be
impeached, although the committee's majority did not formally
recommend it. Clay worried that such an extreme action might
produce a backlash and hurt his chances in 1844. Philip Hone also
thought inaction a better course: "Let [Tyler] serve out his time,
and go back to Virginia, from whence the Whigs have bitter cause
to lament that they ever called him forth." Still, the majority report
was adopted by the House. On August 30, an angry Tyler sent
them a statement, arguing that he was "accused without evidence
and condemned without a hearing. . . . I am charged with violating
pledges which I never gave . . . usurping powers not conferred by
the law, and, above all, with using the powers conferred upon the
President by the Constitution from corrupt motives and for un-
warrantable ends. . . . [T]hese charges are made without any parti-
cle of evidence to sustain them, and, as I solemnly affirm, without
any foundation in truth." He asked that his statement be entered in
the *House Journal*, but the request was refused.[6]

Two weeks later, Congress passed yet another version of the tariff bill, dubbed the "Black Tariff" by its Southern critics, and this

time Tyler signed it into law. There was much in it that he did not like. It is not clear why he gave in, but the desperate need to fill empty government coffers and a desire to prevent impeachment were probably factors. Perhaps he too was exhausted by this endless wrangling, which coincided with another, more painful crisis: his beloved wife was dying.[7]

Letitia Tyler had never recovered from the stroke she suffered in 1839. In July 1842, Tyler told his eldest daughter, Mary, that her mother's "mind is greatly prostrated by her disease," and during the following month she grew weaker. On September 10, she died.

She was the first First Lady to die, and the White House was draped in mourning and the East Room service on September 12 was large and appropriately dignified. The Reverend William Hawley, who seventeen months earlier had conducted the funeral of President Harrison, again officiated. The cabinet attended as did members of Congress, regardless of their party affiliations. President Tyler, accompanied by his family and administration officials and staff, returned Letitia's remains to Virginia. On September 13, with Richmond's bells tolling, the procession proceeded to Cedar Grove, her childhood home and the site of their marriage. As her coffin was lowered into the earth, people cried, "Oh, the poor have lost a friend."[8]

Tyler's sons, daughters, and grandchildren tried to console him, but they could not ease his grief. "Nothing can exceed the loneliness of this large and gloomy mansion—hung with black—its walls echoing our sighs," Priscilla Cooper Tyler observed. During the month of mourning that followed, the Whig press refrained from attacking the president and, with uncharacteristic grace, praised the late Mrs. Tyler as an "estimable lady . . . kind and charitable," loved and respected by all who knew her.[9]

. . .

Letitia's death overshadowed Tyler's first major achievement as president: the successful negotiation of the Washington Treaty, which was approved by the Senate on August 20. The treaty settled several outstanding issues between the United States and Great Britain, whose relations since the 1830s had become seriously troubled.

For Americans, Britain remained the great international bogeyman. In the years following the War of 1812, Britain's international power and wealth had continued to grow and its navy stood as the greatest in the world. New Englanders felt especially vulnerable given the presence of British troops in Canada, which shared a disputed border with Maine. When a rebellion against Great Britain erupted in Canada in the late 1830s, Americans had sympathized with the rebels, and citizens from Vermont to Michigan actively joined the fight. The British crushed the revolt, but tensions still ran high.[10]

In December 1837, British partisans, armed with pistols, pikes, and cutlasses, had attacked and boarded the *Caroline*, an American steamer in New York waters known to have carried arms to the Canadian insurgents. In the fight that ensued, three partisans were wounded and one American died, apparently from a stray bullet. Passengers and crew were escorted safely to shore, and the battle, such as it was, ended ten minutes after it began. Then the British set the *Caroline* afire and the ship slowly sank. New Yorkers were enraged, and local newspapers exaggerated the event, calling it a massacre during which two dozen American innocents were slaughtered. The *Livingston Register* called for "Blood for Blood" until the nation's honor was restored. President Martin Van Buren had sent General Winfield Scott, dressed in full military regalia, to the New York–Canadian border and the immediate crisis ended without further bloodshed. But the British never apologized or compensated the *Caroline*'s owners for the loss of their vessel, and Americans cried "Remember the *Caroline*" and waited for the next incident.[11]

Their wait ended in the winter of 1837–38, in the Aroostook River Valley, part of the disputed territory that pitted Maine against New Brunswick. The Treaty of Paris, which ended the Revolutionary War with Great Britain, left unresolved the line that separated the northeastern boundary of Maine. The dispute was later submitted to the king of the Netherlands, who issued a compromise that the British accepted but the U.S. Senate rejected. Later attempts at mediation had also failed, and that winter new problems arose. Americans who were settling in the area noticed British interest in a road running through the Aroostook Valley, a safe supply route to reinforce Quebec and Montreal, if military necessity so required. "Britannia shall not rule the Maine," went one American tune,

> Nor shall she rule the water;
> They've sung that song full long enough
> Much longer than they oughter.

Canadians and the Americans again prepared for battle.

The "Aroostook War" was mostly one of words. Nova Scotia's legislature appropriated funds in case fighting broke out, and Congress authorized President Van Buren to call for fifty thousand volunteers (the regular army then numbered only seven thousand men) and backed them up with $10 million. "If war must come," proclaimed Pennsylvania senator James Buchanan, "it will find the country unanimous. . . . The only alternative is war or national dishonor; and between these two, what American can hesitate?"

The American who hesitated was the president, who again sent his peacemaker General Scott. After a year's hard work, he arranged a truce in March 1839. But the underlying cause of the crisis—the contested border between Maine and New Brunswick—remained a dangerous irritant between America and Britain.[12]

In November 1840, the *Caroline* affair erupted anew when Alexander McLeod, a Canadian deputy sheriff believed to have been involved in the attack on the ship, was arrested in New York and put on trial for arson and murder. The British strongly protested and informed their minister in Washington that if McLeod was executed it would "produce war, war immediate and frightful." They could not understand why the U.S. federal government would not intervene in a state's judicial proceeding. Almost a year had passed before McLeod was acquitted and the crisis was calmed for the time being.[13]

Tyler inherited these "sticks of dynamite waiting to explode." "The peace of the country when I reached Washington on the 6th day of April, 1841, was suspended by a thread," he later observed. Then, a new crisis occurred in November. Nineteen slaves imprisoned on the *Creole*, an American ship bound for the slave markets of New Orleans, rebelled. They murdered slave owner John Hewell, beat the captain and several of his crew, and forced the *Creole* to sail to Nassau, in the British Bahamas. There, officials bound by Great Britain's Emancipation Act of 1833, which had abolished slavery, eventually freed all the slaves on board, including the rebellion's leader, Madison Washington. Southerners were especially angry; Mississippi newspapers suggested that if the United States failed to protect American "property," there was little reason for any state to remain in the Union.[14]

In response, Tyler asked Congress to increase military appropriations to an astonishing $2.2 million and to begin rebuilding the U.S. Navy. The president "is very sore and testy about the *Creole*," a British official noted. Not only did British interference vex the president; the incident intensified the clash between slaveholders and abolitionists that Tyler wanted to quell. (One abolitionist, perturbed by the administration's initial response to the crisis, called Tyler "an imbecile" and Secretary of State Webster "a poor debauchee.") Although Tyler detested the British, he hoped for a peaceful resolution to the inflammatory issues and he was encouraged by a change in British politics that brought to power a more pacific government. In early 1842, the new Foreign Office sent Alexander Baring, the First Baron Ashburton, to Washington to negotiate a settlement and prevent war.[15]

From the American perspective, Lord Ashburton could not have been a better choice. Not only was he the retired head of the prominent British mercantile firm Baring Brothers and Company, which had financed the Louisiana Purchase, he owned over a million acres in Maine that would surely be threatened by a war. His wife, Anne, was Philadelphia-born and the daughter of former U.S. senator William Bingham. Furthermore, Ashburton had employed Daniel Webster as Baring Brothers' U.S. representative and he and Lady Ashburton considered Webster a good friend; indeed, Webster and his wife had stayed with the Barings during a visit to London three years earlier. When Ashburton was appointed "Commissioner Procurator and Plentipotentiary," Anne Baring wrote Webster that her husband was well known for being "most zealous" about America's interests. "If you don't like him," she added, "we can send you nothing better."[16]

Webster badly needed a victory, something to prove his worth to those Whigs who felt he had betrayed them by remaining in Tyler's cabinet. He was also an Anglophile, as witnessed by visitors to his Washington home, Swan House, which was decorated with portraits of Queen Victoria, the Duke of Wellington, and Lord Melbourne. Webster predicted a quick success, telling Philip Hone that "he had the fullest confidence in being able to settle *all* the differences with England by September." During the negotiations that ensued, Webster kept the president fully informed. With his domestic initiatives blocked by an intransigent Congress, Tyler enjoyed the freedom that foreign policy gave him.[17]

Prior to the start of the talks, Webster concluded that something had to be done to win the support of Maine's citizens. First, he invited both the Maine and Massachusetts legislatures to send representatives—called "commissioners"—to Washington to participate. More troubling, however, the secretary, with Tyler's knowledge and approval, sent to Maine "secret agents," bought and paid for by the government, to "prepare public opinion for a compromise." Among the group was Jared Sparks, a Harvard historian whose research in French archives had turned up a map thought to belong to Benjamin Franklin, one of the negotiators of the Treaty of Paris of 1783. The map seemed to support Britain's claims to the Maine territory. Sparks, at Webster's direction, met with officials of Maine and Massachusetts who, after studying the map, were told that half a loaf was better than none. For his services, Sparks received $250 from the secret service fund; Webster's chief organizer, a Maine politico and publisher named Francis O. J. Smith, received $12,000. Ashburton paid assorted propagandists a total of about $14,500.[18]

The "secret service contingency fund" had originally been requested by President George Washington in 1789, to be used "for the contingent expenses of intercourse between the United States and foreign nations." By 1791, 10 percent of the federal budget was earmarked for the president's secret use. In 1810, Congress established a similar fund hidden in the State Department. Washington and his successors dipped into it to obtain foreign intelligence or, in the case of Jefferson and Madison, to subvert foreign governments in the Barbary States and Spanish Florida. Besides trying to influence opinion in Maine, Webster sent agents to disrupt the activities of the "Patriot Hunters," a radical American group hoping to oust the British from Canada, and the scheme seems to have been the first time that Americans were targets of their own government. These covert agents may only have propagandized—planting articles entitled "Northeastern Boundary—Why Not Settle It?" in newspapers and meeting with state legislators—but for a president who had morally opposed Jackson's imperial presidency, Tyler was skating on the edge of legality. Indeed, in 1846, after both Tyler and Webster left office, the House of Representatives launched an investigation to determine if the secretary was guilty of "official misconduct" in using funds to influence public opinion in Maine. Tyler rejected the charges and most House members accepted his view that the crisis in Anglo-American relations required this extraordinary action. Those who disagreed wondered if such improper activities were unconstitutional and rose to the level of an impeachable offense. Historian Edward Crapol will not let Tyler off easily. "[I]n this quest for personal vindication and political glory," he wrote, "John Tyler betrayed and abused his most deeply held principles."[19]

Lord Ashburton and his party arrived in Washington in early April 1842. The first anniversary of President Harrison's death was being observed throughout the country. In New York, Whig gover-

nor William Seward ordered flags flown at half-staff and bells rung.
The day also provided Whigs with another opportunity to lament
the Tyler presidency. "One year of the rule of imbecility, arrogance,
and prejudice," Hone bemoaned. Ashburton was concerned about
the "strange Confused state of government" he observed in
Washington—Tyler's continuing vetoes and the strength of Whig
vengeance suggested that perhaps no lasting peace could be
achieved. America was "a wild beast," suffering from "ungovernable
and unmanageable anarchy." To Ashburton, Tyler seemed "weak
and conceited." Nevertheless, he warned the Foreign Office "not to
mistake or undervalue the power of this country," which, in the
case of war, would be "immense."[20]

Tyler eventually won him. The president made sure Ashburton
and his associates had comfortable quarters and were wined and
dined. During one week in June, Ashburton attended a wedding
reception, for the late president James Monroe's granddaughter,
where the wine flowed so freely that the next day John Quincy
Adams complained of being hungover. On June 12, there was a
White House gala at which Ashburton enjoyed "dancing in the
now gorgeously furnished East Room and an elegant supper,"
Adams observed. "The courtesies of the President . . . to the guests
were all that the most accomplished European court could have
displayed"—high praise from a man who still considered Tyler "the
Accidental President."[21]

At first, the Webster-Ashburton discussions went smoothly. The
two men agreed to focus primarily on the border dispute in the
northeast (avoiding a similar entanglement in the Oregon territory) and to communicate informally, without diplomatic protocol;
no one kept minutes and nothing would be recorded on paper until an agreement was reached. Despite Webster's efforts to influence public opinion in Maine, its citizens posed the greatest
problem. The state's commissioners, and those of Massachusetts
who stood to profit from the agreement, initially refused to accept
a compromise negotiated by Webster and Ashburton. As the talks
dragged on through an oppressive Washington summer, Ashburton

turned to Webster for help. "I must throw myself on your compassion," he wrote the secretary in July. "I contrive to crawl about in this heat by day & and to live my nights in a sleepless fever. . . . I shall positively not outlive this affair if it is to be much prolonged."[22]

At this point, Tyler stepped in to encourage Ashburton to press on. At a meeting in the president's office, Tyler displayed his celebrated charm, telling the sixty-seven-year-old diplomat that should he go home, all would be lost. "My Lord," said Tyler, according to an observer, "I cannot suppose that a man of your lordship's age and personal position, retired into the bosom of your family after a long and successful life, would have crossed the Atlantic on so arduous a mission, unless you had truly come with the most painful desire to close the unhappy controversies that now threaten the peace. . . . [I]f you cannot settle them, what man in England can?" Having been called indispensable by the president of the United States had its effect. "Well! well!" Ashburton replied. "Mr. President, we must try again." The discussions continued until August 9, when a treaty was signed.[23]

By the terms of the treaty, the border between Maine and Canada was adjusted along the compromise line. The United States received seven thousand square miles of the disputed territory, Britain the remaining five thousand (which included the needed military route to defend Quebec). Ashburton conceded to the United States Britain's claim to two hundred square miles at the head of the Connecticut River and accepted New York and Vermont's borders at the forty-fifth parallel. When the value of the real estate is considered, it is clear that the United States received the better end of the bargain: those seven thousand square miles, it was later learned, held some of the richest iron-ore deposits in the northeast—minerals that would fuel American industry in years to come. To sweeten the deal for those states that lost territory, Maine and Massachusetts were each awarded $125,000.[24]

Other issues were also resolved. The British fought to protect their right to stop and search vessels believed to be involved in the

African slave trade. To Tyler and most Americans, that practice smacked of impressment, one of the issues that had caused the War of 1812. Tyler's answer was a system by which each nation would police the high seas, and, if the opportunity arose, act in concert against slave traders. In the case of the *Creole*, the British agreed not to interfere with American vessels driven into their colonies' ports by bad weather or mutineers. Eventually, the Anglo-American Mixed Claims Commission paid American slave owners more than $100,000 for the loss of their "property." As for impressment itself, Ashburton promised in an informal declaration that Britain would refrain from stopping American ships to search for British citizens, although they refused to officially renounce the practice. The treaty also revised the law of extradition, describing more specifically what crimes would be covered, "including murder, arson, robbery, forgery, and piracy"; those accused would be returned to the country of birth. Finally, Ashburton commented on the *Caroline* affair. He expressed "regret" for the sacking of the *Caroline*, and, though it was not the apology that Americans wanted, Tyler accepted it.[25]

While all the major participants were generally happy with the treaty, winning the required two-thirds majority of the Senate was not a foregone conclusion. Over Webster's opposition, Tyler ordered the entire treaty submitted, rather than each of the individual twelve articles, which he believed would invite rejection. Democrats Thomas Hart Benton and James Buchanan attacked the treaty, condemning Webster for "needlessly and shamefully" giving away so much territory to the British. The treaty was "a solemn bamboozlement," Benton complained.[26]

Senator William Cabell Rives, the chairman of the Foreign Relations Committee, argued for the president. In an executive session, he showed his colleagues the Sparks map, which indicated how much territory the United States had gained. Senator John C. Calhoun then delivered a speech supporting the treaty and converted some critics. "Peace is the first of our wants in the present condition of our country," he said. "If we have not gained all that could be desired, we have gained much that is desirable, and if all has not been settled, much has been." When the final vote was tallied on August 20, 1842, the treaty passed overwhelmingly, with only eight Democrats and one lone Louisiana Whig dissenting. "The work is done, 39 to 9!" a shocked Daniel Webster remarked. Never before in American history had a treaty passed the Senate by so great a majority.[27]

The Treaty of Washington—better known to later generations as the Webster-Ashburton Treaty—was extremely popular in America but it did not help Tyler politically. Democrats remained cool and Whigs refused to applaud him. At a dinner honoring Lord Ashburton prior to his departure for London, one New York Whig proposed a toast to the president. The room plunged into a "dead . . . [and] ominous silence." Even Philip Hone, who often complained of "the faithless and wayward conduct of Mr. Accidental President Tyler," was shocked by such disrespect for the office of the presidency. The next toast—to Queen Victoria—was received enthusiastically.[28]

Tyler's partners in the negotiations treated him better. Webster appreciated the president's "steady support and confidence" and "his anxious and intelligent attention to what was in progress." Writing to Tyler on August 24, Webster said, "I shall never speak of this negotiation, my dear sir, which I believe is destined to make some figure in the history of the country, without doing you justice." The president appreciated the remarks but did not need them: he was proud of his achievement. That peace which had been suspended by a thread when he took office had been transformed, he later observed, into "a chain cable of sufficient strength to render that peace secure."[29]

Tyler was not content merely to settle old boundary disputes. As a graduate of Bishop Madison's school of "empire and national destiny," he had long dreamed of an America that stretched from sea to shining sea, "walking on the waves of the mighty deep . . . overturning the strong places of despotism, and restoring to man his long lost rights." To further continental expansion, Tyler authorized the Department of the Navy to secretly pay a private firm to transport American settlers to the Oregon territory, then jointly occupied by the United States and Great Britain. As Crapol argued, the move was another exhibition of Tyler's habit of using presidential power "in foreign relations without legislative sanction or approval." Similarly, Tyler hoped to enlist British help in convincing the Mexican government to cede California, or at least the important ports of San Francisco and Monterey, to the United States. Neither the British nor the Mexicans were interested, but that did not deter Tyler from sending another secret agent to London to settle the Oregon question and reopen discussions with the Mexicans. That mission failed too.[30]

His Pacific ventures proved more successful. Responding to the entreaties of missionaries and businessmen, in December 1842 Tyler proclaimed that if any foreign power tried to "take possession of the Sandwich Islands, colonize them, and subvert the native Government," they must reckon with the United States. Tyler's sweeping expansion of American influence in the Pacific became known as the Tyler Doctrine. The president also had "his eye fixed upon China" and sent the first official envoy, Caleb Cushing, to open the Celestial Kingdom to U.S. trade. When Tyler learned that Cushing had negotiated the Treaty of Wangxia, opening five Chinese ports to American merchants and granting businessmen and missionaries protection under extraterritoriality, the news sent him "off in an ecstasy." He hoped for a similar relationship with Japan, but his instructions to Cushing did not arrive before he ended his Asian mission.[31]

. . .

Despite these triumphs on the international stage, Tyler remained a lonely, unhappy man. Time did not heal the wound of Letitia's death, and visitors to the White House during the December congressional and social season noticed the gloom that hung everywhere. The First Family was still in mourning, so no lavish White House parties were scheduled.

Later that month, however, Tyler's depression began to lift when twenty-two-year-old Julia Gardiner arrived in Washington and took the city by storm. He was immediately taken with the petite, "buxom dark eyed beauty." Julia was accompanied by her father, David Gardiner, a lawyer and briefly a New York state senator; her mother, Juliana; and her twenty-year-old sister, Margaret. The Gardiners were Eastern aristocrats, wealthy and powerful, longtime residents of Gardiners Island, a large and lavish private estate of 3,300 acres located off the coast of eastern Long Island. Julia and Margaret were educated at Madame N. D. Chagary's Institute for Young Ladies, a fashionable boarding school in Manhattan, but were more interested in New York society than in studying French or mathematics. In late 1839, Julia had shocked New York's social set (and her parents) by posing for an advertisement publicizing Bogert and Mecamly, a clothing establishment located on Ninth Avenue. It was perhaps the first society endorsement for such a business in the city's history: "I'll purchase at Bogert and Mecamly's," said the sign Julia carried in the picture. "Their goods are Beautiful and Astonishingly cheap." The city's "finest" viewed Julia as "cheap" too, once it became known that the pictured woman was David and Juliana Gardiner's eldest daughter. More scandal followed. A few months later, a long and lachrymose poem dedicated to Julia, "Rose of Long Island," appeared on the *Brooklyn Daily*'s front page. "She stole my heart that luckless night," wrote its author, Romeo Ringdove. Julia claimed that she did not know the pseudonymous poet, but her parents were not appeased.[32]

David Gardiner decided it was a good time for the family to tour Europe. They departed in September 1841, and during the following year they met Queen Victoria, whose royal style impressed Julia; King Louis-Philippe of France, who took an instant liking to her; and the pope. Everywhere Julia went she attracted wealthy and titled suitors—barons, counts, government officials. Julia's older brother, Alexander, kept the family informed of the extraordinary political events then occurring in Washington—the war between Henry Clay and John Tyler chief among them. Since they were running out of countries to see, and Julia was leaving a

trail of broken hearts along the way, the family patriarch decided
to return home in September 1842. They scheduled a visit to the
capital in December.[33]

The Gardiners rented rooms at Mrs. Peyton's Boarding House
on Pennsylvania Avenue and had their servant deliver calling cards
to the White House. Julia seemed to be everywhere at once. She
and Margaret could be found in the House of Representatives
gallery, where they entertained their friends and watched "the orators of the day" while they "jumped and screamed and perspired
and foamed and as usual made much ado about nothing." One
newspaper noted that Julia was constantly surrounded by congressmen, "grave Senators not too old to feel the power of youth and
beauty, Judges, officers of the Army and Navy, all vying with each
other to do homage to the influence of her charm."[34]

It was John Tyler Jr., his marriage about to dissolve, who invited
Julia and her family to the White House for a small Christmas Eve
dinner. If she noticed the president, Julia did not remark on it as
her attention was monopolized by John Jr. "He laid quite a siege to
my heart," she observed. On January 2, at another White House occasion, she met "his majesty" the president, who she feared would
not remember her. No man who saw Julia Gardiner ever forgot her,
and John Tyler was no exception. "I hope you are very well," the
president told Julia, taking her hand; Julia was getting over a cold
and was amazed that Tyler was aware of it. In a poem Tyler later
wrote, he confessed to being attracted to Julia's "raven tresses" and
"eyes . . . which beamed as bright as stars."[35]

Julia and the president became especially close at an intimate
White House gathering on February 7, 1843. Tyler flirted with
both Gardiner sisters, but asked Julia to join him alone for a game
of whist. When it was time to leave, the president first kissed Margaret's hand and then approached Julia, who, playing the coquette,
turned away and raced down the stairs. The president, dodging
chairs and tables, ran after her. Margaret thought it "truly amusing,"
but to those who knew Tyler, such behavior was entirely uncharacteristic, so different from the younger man who refrained from

kissing his first wife until just before they wed. Tyler, in a juvenile frolic, apparently did not care who saw him. At a Washington's Birthday ball on February 22, 1843, he asked Julia to marry him. "I had never thought of love," she later noted, "so I said 'No, no, no,' and shook my head with each word, which flung the tassel of my Greek cap into his face with every move. It was undignified but it amused me very much to see his expression as he tried to make love to me and the tassel brushed his face."

Julia's hesitancy might be explained by fear of how her parents would react to the news that she could become the wife of a man thirty years her senior, older even than her own mother. And there were other suitors, including fifty-seven-year-old Supreme Court associate justice John McLean; South Carolina congressman Francis W. Pickens, a widower with four children; and midshipman Richard W. Waldron, a mere twenty-three years old. Learning that the Gardiners intended to leave Washington, Tyler again proposed, hoping he and Julia could be wed in November, prior to the opening of the next Congress and the start of the social season. In Margaret's presence, he talked openly "of resigning the Presidential chair or at least sharing it with J[ulia]," anything to win her heart. But Julia remained uncertain and when her mother, who was concerned that Tyler was not wealthy enough to provide for her, demanded that Julia wait until she knew how she really felt about the president, Julia agreed. She and her family returned to New York in late March as planned.[36]

With Julia gone, Tyler turned to the other "great object of his ambition," the acquisition of Texas. Its annexation, Tyler believed, "shall crown off my public life . . . I shall neither retire ignominiously nor be soon forgotten."[37]

6

The Luster

George Ticknor was worried. The scholar and former Harvard professor was reading articles in the press claiming that the Tyler administration was secretly arranging to bring Texas into the Union. If true, Ticknor feared it would lead to war with Mexico and so exacerbate sectional tensions that America itself might be torn apart. In mid-March 1844, he ran into an old friend on Boston's State Street, former secretary of state Daniel Webster, who had finally left Tyler's increasingly un-Whig-like government in May 1843. After a convivial meeting, Ticknor became serious, asking Webster if what he had read about Tyler and Texas was true. Webster tightly gripped Ticknor's arm and said, "in a low tone but with great emphasis, 'That is not a matter to be talked about in the street; come to me this evening at Mr. Paige's, and I will tell you all about it.'"

When Ticknor arrived at Paige's Boarding House that evening, he found Webster still mysterious and deeply troubled. "It is a long story," Webster said. "I must make a speech to you about it." He had just returned from Washington, where he had met with Abel P. Upshur, the new secretary of state, who complained to Webster about his job and admitted that he would leave were it not for one "particular object" Upshur wanted to "accomplish." Upshur did not explain, but Webster thought he knew what Upshur would not reveal. "I felt Texas go through me," he told Ticknor. Meeting with others in the capital, Webster quickly learned "all about it." He was shocked "at the boldness of the Government," which was, in fact, secretly negotiating with the Texans, offering to protect them from Mexican retaliation. Where this left the Constitution was anybody's guess.

"We might . . . be in a war with Mexico at any time," Webster continued, "with or without the authority of Congress." Indeed it was almost "inevitable," and Tyler seemed "willing to have such a war," which Webster believed would "endanger the Union." Ticknor had never seen Webster so upset: "He became very excited. He walked up and down the room fast and uneasily. He said he had not been able to sleep at night, and that he could think of little else during the day." He urged Ticknor to meet with the city's Whigs, both to see what he could learn and to determine if they were ready to openly combat this terrible prospect.[1]

Time proved Webster right. Just a few months after his meeting with Ticknor, it was widely reported that a treaty annexing Texas was signed and would be submitted for ratification to the Senate.

• • •

U.S. presidents had their sights set on Texas long before Tyler came to power. In 1825, John Quincy Adams tried to buy part of the territory, but Mexico would not sell. Andrew Jackson made an attempt in 1829, but he failed too, and when his minister Anthony Butler (whom Jackson privately called "a scamp") continued to meddle in Mexican affairs, the Mexican government expelled him in 1830. The Texas revolt in 1835 attracted American support, which intensified following Mexican atrocities at the Alamo and Goliad and Sam Houston's surprising victory over General Antonio López de Santa Anna at the Battle of San Jacinto. Americans donated cash to the cause, organized rallies, and volunteered to fight alongside their Texas brothers, "bone of our bone, flesh of our flesh," said one sympathetic congressman.[2]

But when Texas won its independence in 1836 and offered itself to the United States, President Jackson hesitated. The reason was slavery, which was legal and flourishing in Texas. Jackson realized that annexing Texas might bring the country near the breaking point. Northerners strongly opposed admitting Texas, and eight state legislatures sent Congress petitions warning against such action. Abolitionists, believing that the Texas revolution was simply a plot hatched by Southern slave owners, added their voices. William Lloyd Garrison, their most eloquent spokesman, called Texas "the ark of safety to swindlers, gamblers, robbers and rogues" who only wanted to "extend and perpetuate the most frightful form of servitude the world has ever known and add crime to crime." Southerners overwhelmingly called for annexation, seeing it as a once-in-a-lifetime opportunity to divide Texas into five slave states, thereby immensely increasing their power over national politics. As much as Jackson wanted Texas, he would not pay the price of a war abroad or at home.[3]

It was also a presidential election year, and if Jackson accepted Texas's request it might tear the Democratic Party apart and deny the presidency to Martin Van Buren. So Jackson waited until after Van Buren was safely elected, and on his last day in office he formally recognized Texas's independence. Van Buren proved equally cautious. Ending the Panic of 1837 was his chief objective. And on foreign policy he already faced the pesky Maine boundary dispute, so in 1837 he rejected the Texans' renewed request for annexation. Americans, preoccupied by their own economic woes, had no taste for expansion, and were content with the status quo. For the next several years, Texas languished, a separate nation on the borders of the United States.[4]

Spurned by the Americans, the Republic of Texas went abroad in search of allies. Its ambassadors received a warm reception in France and especially in Great Britain. For the British, a thriving, independent Texas served many purposes. Strategically, it would block the United States' further continental expansion while providing a protective barrier for British colonies in the western hemisphere. Economically, Texas cotton would free Britain from dependence on the American South, which had been cut off from trade during the War of 1812. Morally, British abolitionists hoped that the Texans would eliminate slavery, guiding its northern neighbor to emancipation. For the moment, however, all the British (and the French) would offer were treaties of "amity and commerce," but it was still enough to feed American Anglophobia.

Where Jackson and Van Buren feared to tread—annexing Texas—Tyler was eager to go. It was the accidental president, historian Joel H. Sibley noted, who "unexpectedly took up what appeared to be a moribund political matter and succeeded in moving it to the center of the nation's attention."[5]

. . .

Tyler's ambitions for Texas, though keen, at first took a backseat to other, more pressing problems. He expressed interest in annexing Texas early in his administration, first in a conversation with Webster, then again several months later: "[C]ould anything throw so bright a luster around us?" he wrote Webster in October 1841. "I really believe [that] it could be done." But Webster, like most Northern Whigs, opposed annexation, and Tyler, faced with crises at home and abroad, decided that the time was not right to move forward. Indeed, though Texas president Sam Houston twice invited the United States to annex Texas in 1842, Tyler turned him down. "I wish to annex you," Tyler told a Texas emissary, "*but you see how I am situated.*" Nevertheless, the president slowly positioned himself to achieve his goal. He appointed Waddy Thompson, an ardent annexationist, to be U.S. minister to Mexico and dispatched Duff Green, a Calhounite whom John Quincy Adams called the "ambassador of Slavery," to Europe, where he would watch for British attentions toward Texas.[6]

By mid-1843, the administration's achievements in foreign policy—the Webster-Ashburton Treaty, the Tyler Doctrine, and the opening of China—had demonstrated to Tyler what he could achieve through the vigorous (and secret) exercise of presidential power. He had successfully wielded his veto power to prevent unwise Whig policies from becoming law. He had more confidence in his abilities, and his happier private life also contributed to a sense of personal and political renewal.

The public also seemed tired of political squabbles over banks and tariffs; Manifest Destiny had captured their imagination. "Go to the West," one congressman urged his countrymen, "and see a young man with his mate of eighteen; after the lapse of thirty years, visit him again, and instead of two, you'll find twenty-two. This is what I call the American multiplication table." Many were doing a similar math. Tyler desperately wanted to win election in 1844 and believed that acquiring Texas would earn him favor. "Action is what we want," an impatient president remarked in the spring of 1843, "prompt and decisive action."[7]

As his first act, he moved close friends into key posts in the administration. "I have been so long surrounded by men who now have smiles in their eyes," Tyler noted, "and honey on their tongues, the better to cajole and deceive"—and he was tired of it. Following Webster's resignation, he asked Attorney General Hugh Legaré, upon whom he depended for "calm and unimpassioned counsel," to also serve briefly as interim secretary of state. A month later, he asked his old friend and fellow Virginian Abel Upshur, the former navy secretary, to move to the State Department and he agreed. Tyler and Upshur had much in common besides their native state. Both were born in 1790; they had studied law at the same time in Richmond, rose to be prominent lawyers, and served together in the Virginia House of Delegates. Both owned slaves. Most important, Upshur had a passion for annexing Texas that was even greater than the president's, a view he shared with his close friend John C. Calhoun.

When news of Upshur's appointment reached the Texas chargé in the capital, Isaac Van Zandt, he rejoiced: "It will be one of the best appointments for us. His whole soul is with us. He is an able man and has nerve to act." Succeeding Upshur at the Navy Department was another member of Tyler's "corporal's guard," former Virginia governor and congressman Thomas Gilmer, who had voted to sustain Tyler's vetoes in the House. He too called for immediate annexation of Texas. Other appointees included Democrats and two graduates of the College of William and Mary. Tyler at long last felt at home with his cabinet.[8]

Yet a cabinet was not enough. Next, Tyler tried to build a political machine that would support him. Earlier in his career, he had attacked Andrew Jackson's "spoils system," which rewarded friends and allies with government posts. Now that Tyler was president, he found patronage to be a valuable tool to serve his purposes. The cabinet shuffling was accompanied by the removal of more than a hundred officials throughout the government, from foreign envoys to local postmasters. "We have numberless enemies in office and they should forthwith be made to quit," Tyler wrote Secretary of the Treasury John C. Spencer. "The changes ought to be rapid and extensive and numerous—but we should have some assurances of support by the appointees." Loyal Whig Philip Hone was especially incensed by Tyler's removal of the Philadelphia Collector—"a fine old American gentleman"—along with thirty assistants "for the alleged crime of being friendly to Mr. Clay." In their place, "Tyler Men" appeared.[9]

Tyler planned to outflank the Whigs by gaining support from the Democratic Party or possibly by creating a new party of unhappy Northern Democrats and Southern Whigs. Hoping to steal power from Martin Van Buren's Democratic organization, Tyler chose as his New York representative Mike Walsh, a fiery Irish journalist and politico who voted with his fists. He and his personal gang of thugs (Hone called them "prize fighters and pardoned felons") physically disrupted Whig meetings and could be relied upon to do the administration's dirty work, regardless of the consequences. Walsh, of course, favored Texas annexation.[10]

Every presidential candidate of the day needed a biographer to burnish his image. Tyler found his in Alexander Abell, a journalist, who published *The Life of John Tyler* in 1843. To ensure that the book received wide attention, John Tyler, Jr., demanded that government employees buy "50 or 60 copies of the work to be distributed as you shall think best." Historian Edward Crapol called it "a campaign of blatant political shakedowns." One reader, Henry Huggins of New Haven, Connecticut, liked Abell's book and agreed with the author that Tyler was "a patriot, statesman, and an honest man." In return for his services, Abell was named counsel to Hawaii.[11]

For his signature issue, Tyler chose Texas. A propaganda campaign had succeeded in Maine, so Tyler started one on behalf of the republic. Articles and editorials supporting annexation began to appear in friendly newspapers, and Tyler's supporters in Congress called for action. Although many in his inner circle, such as Upshur, emphasized sectional benefits, Tyler took a more nationalist approach to annexation, downplaying the extension of slavery in favor of other factors. Manifest Destiny dictated the admission of Texas into the United States, which, as Jefferson had believed, needed to expand in order to survive. National security would be protected by preventing Texas from becoming a British satellite. There would be "fertile land for the expansion of agriculture, [and] ports and harbors for American trade." And, for those Northerners unfriendly to slavery, Tyler offered again the theory of diffusion— slave owners leaving the South for opportunities in Texas would weaken the "peculiar institution" until it peacefully disappeared. Lest anyone believe that annexation was a cruel land grab at the expense of powerless Mexico, Tyler also argued that Texas was already American territory, having been a part of the Louisiana Purchase—an assertion that had no factual credibility.[12]

Tyler's campaign was not immediately successful. Abolitionists and their allies, such as John Quincy Adams, denounced the president's rosy view. As early as 1836, the Quaker activist Benjamin Lundy feared that annexation was nothing more than "a long premeditated crusade . . . set on foot by slaveholders, land speculators, etc., with the view of reestablishing, extending, and perpetuating the system of slavery and the slave trade." When Representative Henry Wise, Tyler's close friend, spoke imprudently about how

Texas would "add more weight to [the South's] end of the lever," Adams attacked his "sinister motives" as typical of the "slave power conspiracy."[13]

. . .

In June 1843, Tyler decided to renounce his traditional practice of avoiding political campaigning and take his case to the people. Accompanied by John Jr., Robert, Priscilla, and members of his cabinet, Tyler traveled to Boston to dedicate a memorial commemorating the Battle of Bunker Hill. In Baltimore and Philadelphia, they were met by huge crowds, many of whom had never seen a president. In New Jersey, naval captain Robert Stockton invited Tyler to tour the USS *Princeton*, an innovative vessel that was soon to be completed. Increasing the number of U.S. Navy ships was one of Tyler and Upshur's proudest achievements, and the president told Stockton that he looked forward to the visit. Tyler was also greeted "by twenty-six of the most beautiful girls" Priscilla Tyler "ever saw, dressed in white with wreaths of flowers on their heads." Later, the presidential party drove through the city in four wheeled carriages "drawn by six white horses and accompanied by forty young collegians—each mounted on one of Captain Stockton's splendid race horses."[14]

Their reception in New York City was splendid. When Tyler's steamboat entered the harbor on June 12, he found it filled with ships of all kinds, from "men-at-war to club boats," each beautifully decorated with colorful pennants. Naval vessels fired off presidential salutes, bands played, and a military honor guard welcomed him. Somewhere between one hundred thousand and two hundred thousand people appeared to see "the man without a party." Irish immigrants followed the procession carrying signs that read "Honest John Tyler" and "Justice to Ireland." "Everybody stared at the President much as they would have stared at the Emperor of China," noted one observer. Philip Hone declined to attend the festivities: "I did not choose to pay homage to the man who has deceived his friends, and betrayed those who spent time and money and comfort and lungs to place him where he is."[15]

Tyler was somewhat apprehensive about stopping in Rhode Island. The year before, a rebellion had broken out against the state government, which, acting under the old Crown constitution, restricted voting to only men of property and their sons, thus disqualifying more than half of the voting population. The rebels, led by Thomas Dorr, created their own government and a "People's Constitution," which enfranchised the dispossessed. When the governor asked Tyler for help in crushing the revolt, Tyler felt caught in the middle—he was sympathetic to those unreasonably denied the franchise but he could not allow a recognized government to be overthrown. Tyler told the governor that he would send in troops only as a last resort and urged him to revise the ancient charter and offer the rebels pardons in return for their loyalty. When the crisis worsened, Tyler sent Secretary of War John C. Spencer to Rhode Island to signal that he was prepared to use force and the rebels fled. In April 1843, a new state constitution with more liberal voting rights was adopted, but Tyler worried that lingering bitterness would damage his visit. In the end, he found an "enthusiastic" crowd of well-wishers in Providence. State officials were more reserved—the governor's introduction was only two sentences long—but Tyler replied warmly with some political boilerplate about how Rhode Island's small size mattered less than its "pure and patriotic spirit."[16]

His final destination, Boston, was "a hotbed of abolitionism" where some thought the president might not be welcome. Still, there were crowds and military salutes and "sumptuous" dinners and an elaborate parade in which Tyler again rode in a carriage drawn by six handsome horses. This time he did not have to suffer from the June heat and sat in the shade of an umbrella held by a slave. Was it meant as an intentional insult to his abolitionist critics—Tyler refused to meet with abolitionist Wendell Phillips, who planned to urge the president to free his slaves—or simply a form of comfort he, a Southern white man, had come to expect? The Bunker Hill monument was suitably dedicated and a crowd of one hundred thousand gathered to hear Daniel Webster and the president speak of "One Country, One Constitution, and One Destiny."[17]

The mere appearance of the despised Tyler in his beloved Boston was enough to drive John Quincy Adams to fury. He and the other antislavery congressmen boycotted the events. "What a name in the annals of mankind is Bunker Hill! What a day was the 17th of June, 1775! And what a burlesque upon them by Daniel Webster, and a pilgrimage by John Tyler and his cabinet of slave drivers, to desecrate the solemnity by their presence!" Adams wrote in his diary. "Daniel Webster spouting, and John Tyler's nose, with a shadow outstretching that of the monumental column—how could I have witnessed all this at once, without an unbecoming burst of indignation, or of laughter? Daniel Webster is a heartless traitor to the cause of human freedom; John Tyler is a slave-monger. . . . What have these to do with a dinner in Faneuil Hall, but to swill like swine, and grunt about the rights of man?"[18]

Tyler's offending visit was cut short after Attorney General Hugh Legaré, who had just arrived in Boston to attend the ceremonies, became ill and suddenly died, possibly from appendicitis. Tyler was "devastated." "An excursion commenced in buoyancy and gladness, accompanied by the greetings and huzzas of unnumbered thousands, was terminated in sorrow and mourning," Tyler recalled. The president's party carried Legaré's body to South Carolina, where he was buried, before returning to Washington.[19]

Despite this sad end, Tyler's trip was a success. He found that his rather old-fashioned, patrician style of campaigning still worked in this age of political gimmickry. He tested his political rhetoric— many speeches mentioned Texas and Manifest Destiny—and it was heartily endorsed by the people. In Baltimore, New York, and Boston, he made valuable contacts with business and political leaders who he hoped would be useful in the future. But he was under no illusion that the crowds had come to see him personally: it was the office of the presidency that interested them, not its temporary occupant. He believed that he had a winning issue in Texas, and now he had to deliver on it.

. . .

Tyler's secretary of state, Abel Upshur, was eager to help him in the cause. Upshur was obsessed with Texas. "I do not care to control any measure of policy except this; & I have reason to believe that no person but myself can control it," he told a friend. Over the next several months, Upshur moved along a number of tracks. The propaganda campaign was accelerated, emphasizing the benefits of annexation but also intensifying Americans' fears of Great Britain. Articles entitled "Designs of the British Government" were planted in administration organs such as the *Washington Madisonian* but also in the *New York Herald,* the most popular paper in the nation. Upshur met privately with U.S. senators to determine if the required two-thirds vote might be rallied. To win Northern Democrats, the president promised to support all American claims on the Oregon territory. Tyler's old friend William and Mary law professor Beverley Tucker (who stood to profit financially if Texas was annexed) began drafting a treaty that would be acceptable to the Texans.[20]

Sam Houston was naturally skeptical about the change in American policy toward Texas after Tyler's earlier rejections. For the moment, he was more interested in resolving disputes with Mexico, which refused to recognize Texas independence and continued its violence against the republic. Houston's reluctance led Upshur to work even harder to accede to Texas demands. One stumbling block was Texas's demand for U.S. military protection if Houston signed a treaty. Mexico had informed the United States that annexation might mean war, but Tyler was nevertheless willing to give the Texans that assurance. He wanted Texas, and nothing would stop him—not the Mexicans, not the Senate, not even the Constitution. It was an "incredible role reversal," historian Edward Crapol wrote. "[T]he man who claimed to be a strict constructionist had transformed into a gambler and risk taker who would play fast and loose with constitutional requirements. . . . Tyler apparently would go to any lengths to nab the proverbial brass ring."[21]

By late February 1844, Upshur's work was nearly done. The president approved a verbal agreement protecting Texas from attack, and the other details of annexation—transfer of territory, assumption of state debts, and the like—were mostly settled. A canvas of the Senate indicated that Tyler had or was close to securing the two-thirds vote required for ratification. Such a victory would poise him to win another term—perhaps even a significant place in American history.

Equally buoying was the return of Julia Gardiner to Washington. Julia, her sister, and her father arrived on February 24 just as the Texas deal seemed settled. Tyler had not seen the woman he considered his fiancée for almost a year, but he wrote to her often and "dreamily anticipated" her replies. He called her his "fairy girl" and sent her poems filled with romantic images of "setting suns, [and] stars peeping from behind their veils." Julia often read Tyler's poems to her parents, and her sister sometimes mailed them to her brothers, with a note attached: "[P]romise you won't laugh." On February 27, Tyler and Julia were reunited at a lavish White House party attended by hundreds of capital notables. He visibly brightened in her presence, noted one reporter, and "his thin long figure and prominent proboscis were everywhere amid the throng wheeling in ready obedience to the slightest pull of his tail-coat." Many of the guests were talking excitedly about the following day's historic event—a cruise down the Potomac of the USS *Princeton*, Commander Robert Stockton's new steam-powered warship, the grandest vessel in the American navy. The *Princeton* carried the most powerful cannon ever built, the Peacemaker, capable of firing 228-pound balls at any enemy foolish enough to confront it. Those invited would witness a demonstration of the weapon's might.[22]

Wednesday, February 28, was a perfect day for the voyage at sea. The sky was cloudless, the Potomac calm, and the weather unusually mild for late winter. Stockton planned the events with meticulous care. There would be a luncheon of ham and roast fowl with plenty of wine and imported champagne. The guest list included the capital's most distinguished officials: the president of the United States, his fiancée, her father, and members of the First Family and the cabinet, such as Secretary of State Upshur and Secretary of the Navy Thomas Gilmer; Captain Beverly Kennon, chief of the navy's bureau of construction; important members of Congress and the diplomatic corps; and Dolley Madison, the doyenne of Washington society. All told, more than four hundred people came aboard, and after the usual military salutes from cannon and bands the *Princeton* set sail "with majestic grace" on a course bound for Mount Vernon.

Twice that afternoon, the Peacemaker fired, its great cannonballs floating in the air until landing in the sea miles away. The spectators cheered enthusiastically and the band played "Hail to the Chief." Lunch was served belowdecks promptly at 3:00 p.m. There were numerous toasts—to Captain Stockton, to the navy, to so many, in fact, that when Secretary Upshur rose to salute the president, he found his bottle empty. He asked that the "dead bodies" be removed so that he could proceed. "There are plenty of living bodies to replace the dead ones," Stockton joked, handing Upshur an unopened bottle. The toast was made and returned by the president, who raised his glass "to the three great guns: the *Princeton*, her commander, and the Peacemaker."

As the ship sailed home, there was a request for one last demonstration of the Peacemaker's awesome power: Mount Vernon was nearby, and it would be a fitting way to honor George Washington's memory. People climbed to the top deck, but Tyler stopped to listen as his son-in-law William Waller burst into a favorite Revolutionary War song. When Waller reached the word "Washington," the Peacemaker roared again, louder this time, and Waller's audience applauded. Suddenly, there was chaos. An officer, dazed and "blackened with powder," rushed into the salon, calling for a surgeon. Then black smoke poured downstairs and the stunned silence was replaced by screams from above.

Julia Gardiner rushed for the stairs but was blocked by the crowd. "Let me go to my father!" she cried.

"My dear child, you can do no good," someone said, trying to console her. "Your father is in heaven." Julia barely heard the voice as she fell to the floor in a faint.

The Peacemaker had exploded, hurling huge chunks of molten iron at those on deck. Mortally wounded were Abel Upshur, his stomach torn apart; Thomas Gilmer, struck in the head by a jagged piece of metal; and David Gardiner, who bled to death after losing his arms and legs. Also dead were Virgil Maxcy, a diplomat, Beverly Kennon, and Armistead, the president's valet. More than twenty others were injured, including Senator Thomas Hart Benton, who was briefly knocked unconscious. Captain Stockton suffered serious burns to his face and scalp. "My God!" he screamed. "Would that I were dead, too." By the time Tyler reached the deck, the smoke had cleared and the signs of the carnage were everywhere: the mutilated dead were covered by flags and blankets, but torn limbs lay about like sticks. Sailors, "blood oozing from their ears and nostrils," wandered aimlessly while the navy's guests, their clothes torn and stained with blood, stood in shocked disbelief. When the president was shown the bodies of Upshur and Gilmer, he wept.

The president remained on board the *Princeton* until the dead were removed, then, cradling a still unconscious Julia in his arms, he made his way carefully down the gangway. Julia awoke, so startled that her shaking body almost sent them both tumbling into the water. Once safely ashore, they went immediately to the White House. "Joy is turned into mourning," Tyler noted. "The morning, so bright and cloudless, is succeeded by an evening of deep gloom and sorrow."[23]

Washington was stunned by the tragedy. Nothing like it had ever happened to America's government in peace or war. Congress adjourned, the White House again wore black crepe, and the East Room, which a few nights before was a place of revelry, became "a sepulchral chamber, cold and silent as the grave." For two days, five flag-draped coffins lay in state and thousands of citizens passed by to pay their respects. (Missing was Armistead, whose coffin was turned over to his family.) For the third time since 1841, the Reverend William Hawley conducted a White House funeral.[24]

Returning from the burial at the congressional cemetery, the president narrowly escaped death once more. On Pennsylvania Avenue, Tyler's carriage horses suddenly bolted. The driver and John Jr. tried to rein in the horses, but nothing slowed them; as they raced through the crowded market district, pedestrians scattered for safety. At Fourteenth Street, a black man, never identified, "stepped out and stopped the team, saving the president from harm for the second time in four days."[25]

For Tyler, life had become a series of endless tragedies: William Henry Harrison's death in 1841; Letitia Tyler's fatal stroke in 1842; Attorney General Hugh Legaré's sudden passing in 1843; and now the death of his fiancée's father and his two most trusted advisors. His own near-death experience carried extra foreboding alongside these losses. Despite his efforts to comfort Julia, she continued to suffer from "an agony of grief." She was plagued by awful dreams of her dead father, and when she awoke she was convinced that he had visited her. She spent many nights waiting for him to reappear. Less than a week after the accident, she left the White House to attend to her father's final interment in East Hampton, her relationship with the president still not clarified. He too was haunted by the *Princeton* disaster: describing that day's terrible events to his brother-in-law, Tyler broke into tears.[26]

Tyler's emotional state may explain his appointment of John C. Calhoun to fill Abel Upshur's post as secretary of state. The apparent handiwork of Tyler's close friend, Virginia congressman Henry Wise, it was one of Tyler's greatest mistakes. Within hours of the *Princeton* tragedy Wise, believing that annexation belonged in "safe Southern hands," concluded that those hands were Calhoun's. He met with South Carolina senator George McDuffie, a Calhoun intimate, to discuss it. McDuffie, believing that Wise had brought an offer directly from the president, passed it on to Calhoun.

When Wise informed Tyler of his talk with McDuffie, the president was shocked. "You are the most extraordinary man I ever saw!" he yelled. "The most willful and wayward, the most incorrigible!" Calhoun would be a terrible choice. Although Tyler and the "cast iron man" were both loyal Southerners and states' rights men, Tyler was no nullifier. He feared that Calhoun's appointment would needlessly antagonize Texas's enemies—Northerners who feared the extension of slavery, radicals in the abolitionist community, and skeptics in the Senate. With Calhoun as secretary of state, annexation would become synonymous with slavery, the obverse of Tyler's efforts to win *national* support for Texas. Furthermore, although Calhoun had recently withdrawn from the 1844 presidential contest, annexing Texas might revive his candidacy. But the deed was done. To withdraw the "offer" would embarrass Calhoun, lose Tyler important Southern support in the Senate, and injure Wise, whose long years of loyal service Tyler appreciated. Tyler sent Calhoun's nomination to the Senate, which confirmed him unanimously.

To salvage the situation, Tyler pushed to complete the final negotiations before Calhoun took office. He met personally with the Texans to expedite matters. Unfortunately, the chief Texas envoy, General James Pinckney Harrison, could not reach Washington before Calhoun was sworn in as secretary of state.[27]

At first, Tyler and Calhoun worked well together. Meeting with the Texans, the new secretary discovered their demand for an even stronger guarantee of U.S. military protection than Upshur's previous assurances. Tyler ordered Calhoun to give it to them. In writing, Calhoun informed the Texas diplomats that the president had ordered the secretary of the navy to dispatch "a strong naval force to concentrate in the gulf of Mexico, to meet any emergency, and that similar orders have been issued by the Secretary of War to move the disposable military forces on our Southwestern frontier for the same purpose." To pay for the naval buildup, Tyler simply drew $100,000 from the secret service contingency fund.

Tyler took no chances; he wanted to acquire Texas, one way or another. He promised that he would "use all the means placed within his power by the Constitution to protect Texas from all foreign invasion." Should the Senate reject the treaty, he would recommend "in the strongest terms" that Texas be annexed through the constitutional provision allowing Congress to admit new states into the Union. These terms satisfied the Texans and, on April 12, 1844, the formal treaty of annexation was prepared and signed, by Calhoun for the United States and Harrison and Van Zandt for Texas. Ten days later, John Quincy Adams wrote in his diary: "This was a memorable day in the annals of the world. The treaty for the annexation of Texas to this Union was this day sent into the Senate; and with it went the freedom of the human race."[28]

7

The Captain's Bride

Tyler's furtive negotiations with the Texans did not remain secret. On April 27, 1844, five days after its submission to the Senate, Ohio senator Benjamin Tappan, an antislavery Democrat, gave the *New York Evening Post* his copy of the treaty and its accompanying documents, and the news quickly spread throughout the country. A short time later, the Senate voted to rebuke executive secrecy by making public its own deliberations on the treaty. Tyler's hope that the Senate would swiftly ratify the treaty was dead and, with it, the treaty itself.[1]

The records contained a number of bombshells—hints of Duff Green's efforts to scare America into annexing Texas before the British did; the security guarantees given to Texas at the risk of war with Mexico; and, most important, a letter from Secretary of State John C. Calhoun to Britain's minister to the United States, Richard Pakenham, which cast the Texas debate in a most disturbing light. In the so-called Pakenham Letter, Calhoun accused the British of encouraging Texas to end slavery and insisted that the South's "peculiar institution" was, in fact, "a political institution, essential to the peace, safety, and prosperity" of the region. Never happier than when he was philosophizing on behalf of slavery, Calhoun argued that science had indisputably shown that Southern slaves suffered from fewer debilitating diseases—"deafness, blindness, insanity, and idiocy"—than free blacks and that they had "improved greatly in every respect, in number, comfort, intelligence and morals." The Pakenham Letter proved the claims of antiannexationists and abolitionists that the Texas question was only about slavery—its expansion and preservation—despite Tyler's protestations to the contrary.[2]

Public disclosure of the treaty had a major impact in this election year. To Philip Hone, it was the sole issue "which regulates all our politics, the pivot on which party spirit moves, and the stepping stone from which Presidential candidates rise, or on which they stumble to rise no more." The Senate's deliberations revealed "a scene of executive usurpation which ought to subject the chief to impeachment, and such of his advisors as remain . . . to disgraceful dismissal from their offices. . . . Clay must beat them all." Henry Clay was more than ready to fight. Assured of the Whig Party nomination, Clay announced on April 27 that he opposed the treaty. "Annexation and war with Mexico are identical," he proclaimed. Instead, he called for "union, peace, and patience." Martin Van Buren, who wished to return to office, faced a more difficult dilemma: the Democratic Party's traditional North-South alliance was fragmenting. Democrats in the West and South were enthusiastic annexationists, while New Yorkers and others in the Northeast were not. Van Buren tried to straddle the issue by opposing the treaty but agreeing to accept Texas annexation if it did not mean war with Mexico, did not exacerbate sectional tensions, and had the clear support of the whole nation.[3]

Tyler, all hope of success nearly gone, had only one option left—to launch his own party and attempt to act as a spoiler in the November presidential contest. Democrats who endorsed annexation would support him, and though a small contingent, they could prove decisive in a close election. On May 27, 1844, Tyler's so-called Democratic-Republican Party, the name a tribute to his beloved Jefferson, held its first (and last) presidential convention, just down the street from the Democratic Party's meeting in Baltimore. The festivities borrowed liberally from Harrison's hard cider campaign of 1840. The delegates—"federal workers with a day off," noted John Seigenthaler—consumed "large supplies of brandy and water and whiskey and gin" while excitedly waving banners reading "Tyler and Texas." Some conventioneers wanted to wait to see if the Democrats nominated someone more to their liking than Tyler, but the majority wanted to act quickly. "Did you not come here to nominate John Tyler?" responded an Ohio supporter. "Why then wait for the action of any other body? We will not wait; we will not allow any other body to steal our thunder, nor permit any other man to steal our pick-axe. They shall not take our vetoes, neither shall they appropriate Texas to their own party uses." Tyler was nominated one hour after the opening gavel was struck; he did not select a running mate.[4]

The Democrats were having a more difficult time choosing their nominee. Despite his front-runner status, Van Buren was blocked from the nomination because he could not garner two-thirds of the party vote. Not until the ninth ballot did the Democrats unite behind James K. Polk, the first "dark horse" presidential candidate. Tyler approved their choice. A slave owner from Tennessee, Polk was a former Speaker of the House and an expansionist. The Democratic Party platform called for "the re-occupation of Oregon and the re-annexation of Texas at the earliest practicable period."

If Tyler stayed in the race, he threatened to draw enough votes from Polk to elect Clay, which handed Tyler an opportunity to secure his legacy. Formally accepting his party's nomination on May 30, he called for the ratification of the treaty and hinted that he might end his candidacy if Texas were allowed to join the Union. "The question with me is between Texas and the presidency," he said. "The latter, even if within my grasp, would not for a moment be permitted to stand in the way of the first. The Democrats . . . are now looking to me for help," he wrote his daughter Mary on June 4. "I can either continue the contest or abandon it with honor." He would hold off a decision until Polk gave him assurances that he would annex Texas and retain some of Tyler's people in office. The accidental president, the man without a party, remained important.[5]

The party conventions hardened partisan opinions. In the Senate, the combatants fought for almost a month before voting on the treaty on June 8, 1844. Every Whig, except one lone Mississippian, and eight of the Democrats (seven from the North and one Westerner, Thomas Hart Benton) voted thirty-five to sixteen to defeat the treaty. "Mr. Tyler's infamous treaty . . . has received its quietus in the Senate," exulted Hone, while John Quincy Adams called the decisive tally a "deliverance" from "All mighty God. May it prove not a mere temporary deliverance."[6]

Adams's prayers were not answered. On June 10, Tyler sent the treaty and its records to the House of Representatives, informing its members that while he preferred to follow the traditional treaty-making practice, he invited Congress to consider alternative means to achieve Texas annexation. However, the House adjourned before taking action.[7]

. . .

Texas and the presidency were not Tyler's only preoccupations. On June 24, the Washington *Madisonian* announced that the president was leaving town for a brief "repose" from his "arduous duties." Late that night, Tyler, his son John Jr., and two political associates arrived by train in New York City and quietly took rooms at the Howard Hotel. D. D. Howard, the hotel's owner, ordered his employees not to talk about the president's presence and prohibited them from leaving the premises that night. The solution to the mystery was known only to a few—John Tyler was getting married.[8]

It is impossible to know when Julia Gardiner finally decided to become Tyler's wife, but there seems little doubt that her father's tragic death influenced her view of the president. "After I lost my father," she wrote, "[h]e seemed to fill the place and to be more agreeable in every way than any younger man ever was or could be." In late April, Tyler had asked Juliana Gardiner for permission to wed her daughter and promised to "advance her happiness by all

and every means in my power." Juliana agreed, but not enthusiastically. Despite Tyler's "high political position, and unsullied private
character," she was still concerned that he would not be able to provide Julia "with all the necessary comforts and elegancies of life."[9]

They married at two o'clock on Wednesday, June 26, at Manhattan's Church of the Ascension. The Episcopal service was brief,
and since the Gardiner family was still in mourning, only Julia's
immediate family attended. The Tyler party consisted only of son
John Jr. and a few close friends. After the ceremony, the bride and
groom lunched at the Gardiner apartment, then boarded a ferry
for a trip around the harbor. Among the warships that saluted them
was the USS *Princeton*. That afternoon, they boarded a train for
Philadelphia, where they spent their wedding night, and arrived in
Washington the next day. "Wherever we stopped, wherever we
went, crowds of people outstripping one another, came to gaze at
the President's bride," Julia wrote her mother. "The secrecy of the
affair is on the tongue and admiration of everyone. Everyone says it
was the best managed thing they ever heard of. The President says
I am the best of diplomatists." A few days later, they set out for
Charles City County, Virginia, where they honeymooned at Tyler's
new plantation, which he had named Sherwood Forest in honor of
Robin Hood, a fellow political outlaw.[10]

The marriage of a sitting president was another first in American history, and the Tyler wedding drew a great deal of attention.
New Yorkers were especially surprised by the news. Alexander
Gardiner wrote his sister: "At the corners of streets, in the public
places and in every drawing room, it is the engrossing theme."
Philip Hone naturally had an opinion: Tyler was "an old fool," he
wrote in his diary, who "flew on the wings of love . . . to the arms
of his expectant bride. . . . The illustrious bridegroom is said to be
fifty-five years of age and looks ten years older, and the bride is a
dashing girl of twenty-two [*sic*]." Another Whig, George Temple-
ton Strong, was equally caustic: "Infatuated old John Tyler was married today to one of those large fleshy Miss Gardiners . . . poor
unfortunate deluded old jackass."[11]

Newspapers, some respectful, some mocking, salivated over the event. The *New York Herald* could not resist comparing the union of Tyler and Gardiner with that of the United States and Texas. "Miss Gardiner is an honor to her sex, and goes decidedly for Tyler and annexation. . . . The President has concluded a treaty of immediate annexation, which will be ratified without the aid of the Senate," the editors noted wryly. "Now, then, is the time to make a grand movement for Tyler's re-election. Neither Polk nor Clay can bring to the White House such beauty, elegance, grace, and high accomplishments." The *Herald* also took a swipe at the *Madisonian's* announced reasons for the president's absence: "We rather think that the President's 'arduous duties' are only beginning. 'Repose,' indeed!"[12]

Reactions in Washington followed party lines. As expected, John Quincy Adams was horrified. "Captain Tyler and his bride are the laughingstock of the city," he noted. "It seems as if he was racing for a prize-banner to the nuptials of the mock—heroic—the sublime and the ridiculous. He has assumed the war power as a prerogative, the veto power as a caprice, the appointing and dismissing power as a fund for bribery; and now, under circumstances of revolting indecency, is performing with a young girl from New York the old fable of January and May." Tyler's friends were somewhat bemused by the thirty years that separated the bride from the groom. When Tyler's friend Henry Wise learned that Tyler planned to marry twenty-four-year-old Julia, he asked, "Have you really won her?"

"Yes," Tyler replied, "and why should I not?"

"You are too far advanced in life to be imprudent in a love scrape," insisted Wise.

"How imprudent?" demanded Tyler.

"Easily. You are not only past middle age, but you are President of the United States, and that is a dazzling dignity which may charm a damsel more than the man she marries."

"Pooh!" exclaimed Tyler. "Why, my dear sir, I am just full in my prime!"[13]

Tyler's family was not amused by the marriage. Although Tyler's

four daughters and three sons were aware of their father's interest
in Julia, only John Jr. knew about the wedding. In fact, it appears
that Tyler intentionally kept them in the dark about the coming
event. On June 4, three weeks before the ceremony, he wrote his
eldest daughter, Mary, and noted that there was "nothing which
would be of any interest to you." Tyler's daughter Elizabeth was
four years younger than Julia and still missed her mother greatly;
for the first three months after they married, she was unable to
write to her stepmother, whom she addressed as "Mrs. Tyler." The
youngest, Alice, was seventeen; she too had difficulty adjusting to
the new woman in her life. While Elizabeth and Alice eventually
accepted Julia, Letitia, named for her mother, did not. The Tyler
men—Robert, John, and Tazewell (only fourteen)—liked Julia in-
stantly and welcomed her.[14]

"I have commenced my auspicious reign," Julia wrote her
mother after returning to Washington, "and am in quiet possession
of the Presidential Mansion." She found her domicile "a disgrace to
the nation," a profound disappointment compared to the family
mansions on Gardiners Island and Lafayette Place. The building's
pillars were more a tobacco-stained brown than white, and the
East Room's chairs were torn and soiled, not fit even for "a brothel."
An earlier request for funds to refurbish the president's home was
rejected by Congress, so the First Lady asked her mother to contribute the needed cash. Juliana was happy to help. "You know how
I detest a dirty house," she told her daughter.[15]

Like all brides, she also found it difficult making the transition
from honeymoon to normal domestic life, but living with the president of the United States presented special problems. According
to Julia, Tyler told her that "the honeymoon is likely to last forever
for he finds himself falling in love with me every day," but he was
too often preoccupied with less romantic affairs of state. Juliana
reminded Julia of her husband's responsibilities and offered advice:
"Business should take the precedence of caressing—reserve your
caressing for private leisure and be sure you let no one see it unless
you wish to be laughed at." Tyler for his part was slow in adjusting

to a woman so different from his first wife, the quiet and reserved Letitia. For all her beauty and charm, Julia sometimes acted like "a spoilt child," Tyler complained. But the period of adjustment ended, and the second Tyler marriage proved to be one of the happiest in presidential history.[16]

* * *

Their first summer together passed quickly. Julia oversaw the White House repairs while Tyler built up the Democratic-Republican Party. The more Tyler could challenge Polk's chances, the more certain he was that Polk would deliver on his promise to annex Texas. He concentrated his chances on three states crucial to the Democrats—New York (where Julia's brother Alexander Gardiner was put in charge), New Jersey, and Pennsylvania. Tyler ruthlessly used patronage to build an organization loyal to "Tyler and Texas." Tyler also believed he had support in Ohio and could carry Virginia for Polk. "Our course is now a plain one," he told his son Robert. "Make these [Polk] men feel the great necessity of our cooperation."[17]

His actions were enough to scare Polk into sending Mississippi senator Robert J. Walker, a pro-annexation conservative, to meet with the president. Tyler told Walker that he hoped Polk would win in November—and that he was willing to help. He claimed to have more than 150,000 dedicated supporters who, at his command, would support "Young Hickory," as Polk's fans were calling him. He asked in return that his allies be allowed to join the Democratic Party and be treated "as brethren and equals." If Polk or his representative could give Tyler that guarantee, he promised to "withdraw" and support Polk enthusiastically. Walker was receptive. He reported to Polk that Tyler's "cooperation cannot be overrated. In my judgment, it would be decisive in your favor." Polk agreed.[18]

All that Polk needed was a mechanism that would allow Tyler to gracefully drop out of the race without reviving suspicions of a "corrupt bargain" like the one that haunted John Quincy Adams after his alliance with Henry Clay. Polk sent his law partner Gideon Jackson Pillow to the Hermitage to confer with former president Andrew Jackson, now ill but still determined to defeat the hated Clay. Jackson thought Tyler was asking too much for a man whose political support amounted "to a mere drop in the bucket," but he recognized the dangers posed by a Tyler candidacy. As the grand old man of the Democratic Party, he offered to write letters assuring Tyler of everything he wanted. None would go directly to Tyler, however. Instead, Jackson wrote to John Y. Mason, Tyler's secretary of the navy and an old friend of Polk's, who was certain to share the correspondence with the president. In this way, the arrangement could be consummated without Polk's or Tyler's direct involvement.

On August 20, Tyler's final campaign message was printed in the friendly *Madisonian*. It announced, "To My Friends Throughout the Union," Tyler's decision to leave the field and defended his record—vetoes and all—as president. He promoted his Texas treaty, emphasizing its national benefits, avoiding Calhoun's emphasis on slavery, and denying that it would cause civil war. "The glory of my country, its safety and prosperity alike depend on Union," he wrote, "and he who would contemplate its destruction, even for a moment, and form plans to accomplish it, deserves the deepest anathemas of the human race." His only remaining ambition was "to add another bright star to the American constellation"; annexing Texas would be "an unfailing source of gratification to the end of my life." Tyler's supporters easily switched their allegiance to Polk, persuading him that a Polk administration would be "a continuation of my own, since he will be found the advocate of most of my measures." And so Tyler became the first incumbent president to decline to seek a second term.[19]

Less than three months later, James K. Polk won the presidency, defeating Henry Clay by a little more than eight thousand votes out of 2.7 million cast. Polk won fifteen states to Clay's eleven; the Whigs lost eight states that Harrison carried in 1840. Because so few votes separated winner from loser, everyone claimed credit for the Democrats' success—the Southern annexationists, the Northern abolitionists, the recently (and often illegally) enfranchised Irish and Germans in New York and Pennsylvania, and last, but not least, the Tyler men. All or none may be correct, but New York was indisputably critical; Polk carried it by five thousand votes, many of them cast by the immigrants. The Whigs had been openly hostile toward these voters, as symbolized in Clay's choice for his vice presidential running mate—Theodore Frelinghuysen, a Protestant reformer with anti-Catholic associations. In addition, Democrats had a rising star in New York gubernatorial candidate Silas Wright, who, despite his opposition to annexation, may have boosted Polk's returns. Texas, it seems, had not influenced voters, but the Democrats—and Tyler—did not realize it, even if their opponents did. As one unhappy Whig later put it, "The election was decided . . . by the people of New York & Pennsylvania, Michigan and Maine [all won by Polk], on considerations and feelings, unconnected with any great national principles or interests."[20]

Tyler interpreted Polk's victory differently. Of the five states he targeted for special attention—New York, New Jersey, Pennsylvania, Ohio, and Virginia—Polk won three, leading Tyler to believe that his case for annexing Texas and his withdrawal had been the decisive factors. He had beaten Henry Clay, the man who had tried but failed to destroy his presidency. "Hurrah for Polk!" Julia cried. "What will become of Henry Clay. . . . We shall have a very pleasant winter here I can now promise." Her husband too was "happy as a clam at high water," but gracious in victory. "Leave off abusing Mr. Clay altogether," he told his supporters in the press. "He is dead and let him rest."[21]

. . .

Although Tyler had less than four months left in the White House, he would not retire quietly. Indeed, because he interpreted Polk's victory to mean there was a national mandate for annexation, he hoped to fulfill his last ambition before Polk's inauguration. In his annual message to the lame-duck Congress on December 4, Tyler declared that "it is the will of both the people and the States that

Texas shall be annexed to the Union promptly." He asked the House and Senate to pass a joint resolution admitting Texas into the Union; only a simple majority in each chamber was required, and his signature. Once again, Tyler's ambition and necessity trumped his earlier fervent constitutional ideology. This time, he had at his side an invaluable ally, "The Lovely Lady Presidentress."

The title was the invention of F. W. Thomas, a *New York Herald* reporter, whom Julia had hired as a press agent. His chief responsibility was "to sound Julia's praises far and near." It was not a hard job. Washington had never quite seen anyone like Julia Gardiner Tyler. Besides being the youngest First Lady in history, she was also the most glamorous and extravagant. Thomas, possibly earning his pay by the word, called her "the most accomplished woman of her age . . . a spirit of youth and poetry and love, and tenderness, and riches, and celebrity, and modesty."[22]

Julia's mother should not have doubted the president's ability to maintain her in the style to which she was accustomed; what Julia wanted, John gave her. He asked the American consul in Naples to select an Italian greyhound to accompany Julia on her daily stroll. She rode through Washington's streets in a carriage pulled by a half dozen Arabian horses. Accused of having contracted a case of "queen fever" during her travels abroad, she installed herself as the White House's social monarch. One reporter described a typical day: "[She] is attended . . . by twelve maids of honor. . . . Her serene loveliness received upon a raised platform wearing a headdress formed of bugles and resembling a crown." She asked that the Marine Band play "Hail to the Chief" whenever her husband appeared at social and official events.[23]

Yet Julia Tyler was interested in more than lavish entertaining; she wanted to be involved in current affairs. Dolley Madison forbade the discussion of political issues at her White House parties ("politics is the business of men," she said), but Julia encouraged it. While her guests danced the polka, a popular European import Julia had introduced to Washington society, she lobbied for Texas. She made certain that copies of the president's December message were distributed throughout the capital. At one dinner, she wiled the public support of Supreme Court Associate Justice John McLean, her former suitor. It was "a matter of honor," she told John C. Calhoun, seated next to her. "There is no honor in politics," a sullen Calhoun replied. She smiled. "We will see." Then Julia wrote down what she wanted McLean to say and passed the note to him. The justice read it, looked at Julia, and said, "for your sake," then raised his glass to "Texas and John Tyler." Tyler was happy to have McLean's help but it "made the President as jealous as you please," Julia's sister Margaret noted.

Such nights were complemented by daily visits to Capitol Hill. "I will make as many friends as I can among the Senators," Julia told her brother Alex. People soon sang of her efforts:

> Texas was the Captain's bride,
> Till a lovelier one he took;
> With Miss Gardiner by his side,
> He, with scorn, on kings, may look.[24]

After debating the Texas issue for five weeks, the House approved 120 to 98 a resolution admitting Texas as a state on Saturday, January 25, 1845. Voting was along party lines, with the Democrats solidly supporting Polk's position in favor of annexing Texas. "Rejoice with me," Tyler exclaimed when he heard the news. "I entertain strong hopes that it will pass the Senate. A greater triumph was never achieved."[25]

But Senate passage, as Philip Hone noted, was "now the great question." Senators, protective of their treaty-making prerogatives, were especially concerned about acquiring foreign territory through a resolution when the Constitution clearly required them to ratify such arrangements. On February 4, the Foreign Relations Committee went on record opposing annexation by resolution. Deadlock was in the offing. "Politically all seems confusion," observed Juliana Gardiner, who, like the entire Tyler-Gardiner clan, was following the developments closely. "One day no doubt of annexation; the next, all doubt."[26]

In mid-February, President-elect Polk arrived in Washington and pressured the Senate to act. "He is for Texas, Texas, Texas," noted one senator, "and talks of but little else." The Whigs despaired. "Texas will be brought into the Union," said Representative Washington Hunt. "There is no escape." Polk's intervention finally produced a compromise, offered by Mississippi senator Robert J. Walker, who would soon be Polk's secretary of the Treasury, that allowed the president to either annex by resolution or reopen treaty negotiations with the Texans. It was a clever stratagem: a few Southern Whigs and Northern Democrats, originally opposed, voted for the final resolution, believing that Polk would choose negotiation and annexation would eventually fall through. Their votes allowed the resolution to pass, twenty-seven to twenty-five. The House approved the Senate version and everyone awaited Polk. Tyler, said South Carolina senator George McDuffie, "would not have the audacity to meddle with [the resolution]."[27]

· · ·

Once again, Washington officialdom underestimated John Tyler. He had no wish to share the glory of Texas with the next president and, fearing that further delay would cause Texas to align itself with Britain or France, he signed the annexation resolution on March 1, three days before leaving office. He later explained his decision to the cabinet, which supported it unanimously, and sent Calhoun to inform Polk, who, while surprised, expressed no opinion. Those observing Tyler affix his signature wondered to whom he would give the coveted pen he had just used to bring Texas into the Union. Would it be Secretary of State John C. Calhoun? Senator Robert J. Walker, breaker of the Senate logjam? No. He gave the "immortal golden pen" to the Lady Presidentress, who wore it proudly around her neck that day and for many days thereafter.

Tyler's bold action pleased the Texans but was not well received by others. John Quincy Adams growled that the Constitution had been made "a menstrous rag." Many Whigs were bereft. "The Goths are in possession of the Capitol," Philip Hone wrote, "and if the Union can stand the shock it will only be another evidence that Divine Providence takes better care of us than we deserve." Also angry were those Democrats who were convinced that the final decision and credit belonged to Polk. "Thus quieted in their apprehensions," said Thomas Hart Benton, "five Senators voted for the act of admission who would not otherwise have done so."[28]

For the Tylers, the campaign for the annexation of Texas was a spectacular final achievement, and they spent their last weeks in the White House celebrating. "President Tyler will go out of the White House with drums beating and colors flying," Julia's publicist announced. In planning her last hurrah, Julia wanted "to do something in the way of entertaining that shall be the admiration and talk of the Washington world." For her final official ball on February 18, she invited two thousand people, but another thousand showed up. "We were as thick as sheep in a pen," Margaret complained, and when dinner was called there was "such a rush, crush, and smash to obtain entrance [as] was never seen before at a presidential entertainment." Later, as the throng danced under "a flood of light" cast by the chandeliers' thousand candles, the president, obviously delighted, remarked, "They cannot say now that I am a President without a party!"[29]

Late on the afternoon of March 3, the Tylers prepared to depart the White House for the last time. John Peter Van Ness, president of the Metropolitan Bank, stepped forward and delivered a brief "farewell address," praising Tyler's service and hoping that when current tempers cooled, he would receive "that justice and praise which he so richly deserved." Then, the president "raised his hand" and began to speak, "his voice . . . more musical than ever," Julia thought. "It rose and fell, and trembled and rose again." He said:

> In 1840 I was called from my farm to undertake the administration of public affairs, and I foresaw that I was called to a bed of thorns. . . . I rely on future history, and on the candid and impartial judgment of my fellow citizens, to award me

the meed due to honest and conscientious purposes to serve
my country.

He recalled the circumstances under which he had come to
power, "almost alone between the two great parties which divide
the country. A few noble-hearted and talented men rallied to my
support . . . a corporal's guard," the group once ridiculed but now
honored. He continued:

> The day has come when a man can feel proud to be an Amer-
> ican citizen. He can stand on the Northeastern boundary or
> on the shores of the Rio Grande del Norte and contemplate
> the extent of our vast and growing Republic, the boundaries
> of which have been settled and extended by peaceful negoti-
> ations. . . . The acquisition of Texas is a measure of the great-
> est importance. Our children's children will live to realize
> the vast benefits conferred on our country by the union of
> Texas with this Republic.

Applause greeted the accidental president and his greatest
achievement. "The effect was irresistible," Julia noted, "and the
deep admiration and respect it elicited was told truly in the sobs
and exclamations all around. As they shook us by the hand when
we entered our carriage they could not utter farewell."

The day was historic in another way: as he left office, Congress
overrode Tyler's last presidential veto. It was on a minor bill author-
izing the construction of two vessels for the Revenue Cutter Service, but Congress had never before been able to amass enough votes
to do it. Tyler's unprecedented presidency ended as it began.[30]

8

No Rest

Tyler's transition to private citizen was at times difficult. At fifty-four, he was the youngest ex-president in history, and emulating his heroes Thomas Jefferson and James Madison, he retired in 1845 to his Virginia plantation, Sherwood Forest, along the James River in Charles City County. Located near Greenway, his ancestral home, the plantation spread across twelve hundred acres. Julia planned to remodel the two-and-a-half-story house, adding a sixty-eight-foot ballroom, among other improvements. "I assure you Mama my house outside and in is very elegant and quite becoming 'a President's Lady,'" Julia wrote her mother, Juliana. "You will think it is a sweet and lovely spot."

At first, Tyler worried that the life provided by a gentleman farmer would disappoint Julia after her exciting eight months in the White House. "The President," as Julia continued to call him, "is puzzling his wits constantly to prevent me from feeling lonely," she told Juliana. "If a long breath happens to escape me he springs up and says 'What will you have,' and 'What shall I do for I am afraid you are going to feel lonely!'" In reality, she was weary of the "routine of gaiety" and enjoyed the "repose" she found at Sherwood Forest.

So did her husband. Tyler planted wheat, corn, grain, and fruits and tended them carefully. At harvest time, he spent three to four hours a day riding through the fields "among the slaves, encouraging them by his presence." He purchased more slaves, bringing the plantation's number to more than seventy. Often Julia would join him late in the afternoon, as the sun went down. They would sit on the piazza, Tyler in a large, comfortable chair, feet up on the railing, reading, while Julia wrote to her mother or her sister. They watched "the reapers come to their labors in the fields," she noted, "their loud merry songs almost drown the President's voice as he talks with me. Once in a while a scream from all hands, dogs and servants, cause[s] us to raise our eyes to see a full chase after a poor little hare." Unlike Washington's Mount Vernon, Jefferson's Monticello, and Madison's Montpelier, which were difficult to restore when each president left office, Tyler's plantation flourished, as did its owners. Tyler had saved a good portion of his annual presidential salary of $25,000 and, along with Julia's sizable inheritance, they lived comfortably. Indeed, they were able to purchase a summer home near the Hampton Roads (named Villa Margaret, after Julia's sister), which provided a refuge from Virginia's malaria outbreaks, and vacationed at resorts at White Sulphur Springs and visited Julia's mother in New York.[1]

At times, though, it was a lonely life. Gone were the numerous visitors who had filled the White House, sometimes to overflowing. Nor was Tyler bothered as were Washington and Jefferson and Jackson by hordes of aspiring politicians who sought advice or endorsements. Tyler was still a political pariah, despised by the Whigs, unwelcomed by the Democrats. Most of his nearest neighbors were Whigs, and the local social set shunned them. Charles City County officers tried to embarrass Tyler by appointing the ex-president "overseer" of the road that ran by his property, but next to Henry Clay, this bunch was easy to outfox. As overseer, Tyler required his neighbors to leave their farms and physically repair the road, even at harvest time and during inclement weather. Tyler's interruptions quickly annoyed them and they demanded that he relinquish his post. This too was child's play for "Old Veto." He told them that "offices were hard to obtain in these times, and having no

assurance that he would ever get another he could not think, under
the circumstances, of resigning." But eventually the couple made
many new friends, who invited them to teas, dances, and dinner
parties.[2]

They settled into a happy life at home. Julia gave birth to seven
children between 1846 and 1860. First to arrive was David Gardiner Tyler, called by family friends the "Little President," who was
born at his grandmother's home in New York. The pleasure of his
arrival was temporarily marred by a rumor circulating through
New York and Washington that David's parents were on the brink
of divorce. Nothing could have been further from the truth: despite the thirty years that separated them, Julia continued to be
"her husband's devoted admirer and a contented and happy wife,"
said one who knew them well. (In fact, it was John Tyler Jr.'s continuing marital woes that had caught the attention of gossip mon-
gers, and the story became garbled as it made the rounds.) Julia
and Tyler's second child, John Alexander, was delivered in 1848,
followed by Julia in 1849, Lachlan in 1851, Lyon in 1853, Robert
Fitzwalter in 1856, and finally Pearl, born in 1860, when Tyler was
almost seventy. To his friend Henry Wise, who had questioned
whether Tyler should marry such a young woman, he said, "You see
how right I was; it was no vain boast when I told you I was in my
prime. I have a houseful of goodly babies budding around me." All
told, Tyler and his two wives produced fifteen children, a presidential record. Tyler, born the year after George Washington was inau-
gurated, produced a family that survived until 1947, when Harry
Truman was president.[3]

. . .

Tyler was undoubtedly happy being a gentleman farmer and new
father. "My old age," he told a friend, "is enlivened by the scenes of
my youth—and these precious buds and blossoms almost persuade
me that the springtime of life is still surrounding me." But, like
many one-term presidents, he had a chronic case of Potomac fever.
Even as he settled at Sherwood Forest in 1845, Tyler kept in touch

with political allies in New York, New Jersey, and Pennsylvania. In the Keystone State, his son Robert helped secure a pro-Tyler newspaper, the *Spirit of the Time*, and reported that his father had more than three thousand supporters.[4]

But Tyler's chances of winning the Democratic nomination in 1848 were significantly weakened by an emboldened President Polk. Although he had pledged to serve only one term, Polk did not want Tyler back in the White House. Soon after taking office, Polk purged hundreds of Tyler appointees from government service. Tyler, believing that he was responsible for Polk's election, was disappointed and angry. "If Polk had played his game wisely," he wrote Robert, "he would have reconsolidated the old Republican Party. . . . Such was my policy; but he destroyed, I fear, all that I built up, by the proscription of my friends." For her part, Julia was thrilled to learn that the new First Lady, Sarah Polk, was a complete failure. Mrs. Polk, a devout Methodist, forbade dancing, drinking, and card playing at the White House, so Julia's presence, if not her husband's, was greatly missed in Washington.[5]

The unlikelihood of another term in the presidency made Tyler more determined to protect the reputation of the one term he had. In May 1846, he returned to Washington to testify before the House Foreign Affairs Committee, which had accused Daniel Webster of bribery and corruption during the 1842 propaganda campaign in Maine. Tyler ably defended his former "premier," and the charges against Webster were dropped. A year later, he confronted another challenge to his legacy. John C. Calhoun suddenly claimed that he himself was chiefly responsible for annexing Texas—"a measure which has so much extended the domains of the Union." Tyler was both piqued and worried by Calhoun's action. "Was there ever anything to surpass in selfishness the assumption of Mr. Calhoun?" he wrote Alexander Gardiner. "He assumes everything to himself, overlooks his associates in the Cabinet, and takes the reins of government into his own hands. . . . He is the great 'I am' and myself and the Cabinet have no voice in the matter." A response was necessary and, at first, Tyler considered writing a memoir or a book about his foreign policy, but then chose to write letters to the *Richmond Enquirer,* which his allies would distribute throughout the country. Tyler could not allow his presidency to be reduced to "a mere Southern agency in place of being what it truly was—the representative of American interests . . . and if ever there was an American question, then Texas was that very question." That seemed to silence the "impudent" Calhoun.[6]

No sooner did Tyler respond to Calhoun's outrageous statements than the Whig press reopened its attacks on the former president. This time, the Whig *Intelligencer* accused Tyler of being the tool of land and stock speculators who would greatly profit from an American Texas. Tyler shot back, claiming that he represented no local, sectional, or private interest but "the glory of the whole country." Actually, the *Intelligencer* was not entirely wrong. While Tyler himself had no economic interests to further ("I never owned a foot of Texas land or a dollar of Texas stock in my life," he insisted), many of his closest associates did, including Secretary of the Navy Thomas Gilmer, who had been killed on the *Princeton,* Attorney General John Y. Mason, secret agent Duff Green, and William and Mary's Beverley Tucker, Tyler's legal advisor on drafting the treaty. Stung by these various accusations, Tyler announced in 1848 that he would not be a candidate for reelection.[7]

These minor squabbles were soon overshadowed by the outbreak of war between the United States and Mexico, a conflict for which Tyler was partly responsible. Two days after Tyler signed the annexation resolution, and while he was still the incumbent president, the Mexican minister asked for his passport and left Washington. On his arrival, Polk was determined both to end the joint British-American occupation of Oregon and to carry America to the Pacific, no matter the cost. The acquisition of the Oregon territory occurred peacefully, but the Mexicans chose to fight. The war began in May 1846 and sixteen months later General Winfield Scott marched triumphantly into Mexico City. "The United States will conquer Mexico," Ralph Waldo Emerson predicted, "but it will be as the man who swallows the arsenic which brings him down.

Mexico will poison us." The five hundred thousand square miles of territory taken from Mexico in settlement included the future states of California, Nevada, Utah, Arizona, and much of New Mexico, and deepened the sectional crisis that led to civil war.

Tyler watched these developments with grim foreboding. Not long after the Mexican War began, Pennsylvania congressman David Wilmot introduced a resolution to prohibit slavery in any territory won from Mexico. Southerners, Tyler among them, were outraged by the Wilmot Proviso. In an anonymous letter to the Portsmouth, Virginia, *Pilot*, Tyler called the measure "nothing less than a gratuitous insult on the slave states." Southern boys were fighting and dying in Mexico, yet Representative Wilmot wanted to deny them the spoils of victory. "You may toil and bleed and pay," Tyler wrote, "and yet your toil, and blood and money shall only be expended to increase [the North's]; you and [the South's] property being forever excluded from the enjoyment of the territory you may conquer." The House passed the resolution but it died in the Senate. Nevertheless, what Tyler termed the "contest between the sections for the balance of power" was unfolding.[8]

In 1850, the fruits of the Mexican War again contested the balance of power. California—even richer because of the recent discovery of gold and its growing population—wished to enter the Union as a free state, and New Mexico and the Oregon territory, similarly inclined, waited in the wings. For Southerners, these were ominous developments alongside the creation in 1848 of the Free Soil Party, dedicated to "free soil, free men, and free labor." The party had chosen as its nominee former president Martin Van Buren, who had siphoned votes from Democrat Lewis Cass to give the election to Whig general Zachary Taylor. "As things now stand," said John C. Calhoun in February 1850, the South "cannot with safety remain in the Union." A dwindling group of Southern moderates looked to the one man who had prevented civil war thirty years earlier—Henry Clay.[9]

With the help of Daniel Webster and Illinois Democrat Stephen A. Douglas, Clay, now seventy-three years old and at the end of his career, cobbled together a congressional package to manage the sensitive sectional issues: California was admitted as a free state; the citizens of the New Mexico and Utah territories were permitted to choose their future status on the basis of popular sovereignty; the slave trade in the District of Columbia was abolished; and a new, strict Fugitive Slave Law gave the federal government the power to pursue and return runaway slaves to their owners. Clay spoke for hours at a time with an eloquence that still dazzled his audience. He asked his countrymen on both sides of the great sectional divide "to pause—solemnly to pause—at the edge of the precipice before the fearful and disastrous leap is taken into the yawning abyss below." Webster added his own great voice: "I speak today for the preservation of the Union. Hear me for my cause."[10]

Southern diehards were opposed. Calhoun, too ill from the tuberculosis that would shortly kill him, was unable to speak; his protest was read to the Senate by Virginia's James M. Mason. In a move that surprised some of his friends, Tyler supported Clay and the "compromise" he offered the nation. In a letter that received wide readership throughout America, the former president endorsed Clay's work. The legislation passed. "There is rejoicing over the land," Philip Hone observed. "The bone is removed; disunion, fanaticism, violence, insurrection are defeated." For once, Tyler and Hone were in hopeful agreement.[11]

• • •

The Compromise of 1850 only delayed what seemed to all inevitable—the breakup of the Union. Sectional violence was unstoppable. In 1854, Senator Stephen A. Douglas put forward the Kansas-Nebraska Act, which permitted new territories to choose to be free or slave states. It won Tyler's support, but violence soon flared between free soilers and slavers who poured into Kansas from Missouri. In May 1856, the town of Lawrence, Kansas—considered "a hotbed of abolitionism"—was attacked by pro-slavery sympathizers, and in revenge John Brown, the abolitionist who wanted to purge "the crimes of this guilty land . . . with Blood," let his Liberty Guards loose on the town of Pottawatomie. They murdered five citizens believed to favor slavery. Eventually, two hundred lost their lives in "Bloody Kansas."[12]

It was Brown who pushed John Tyler toward favoring secession when, in October 1859, he and his Liberty Guards seized the federal arsenal at Harpers Ferry, Virginia. Brown planned to arm the many slaves he expected would join them in rebellion. Instead of a host of grateful slaves, federal troops arrived, commanded by Colonel Robert E. Lee. They captured Brown, who was later tried and convicted of treason against the Commonwealth of Virginia, then hanged. Brown wanted to die a martyr, and at that he succeeded. He was called "an angel of light" by Henry David Thoreau; fellow abolitionist Wendell Phillips proclaimed that the "lesson of the hour is insurrection."[13]

Brown's desperate act, and the support he won from the abolitionists, terrified Virginians, Tyler among them. Blacks outnumbered whites more than two to one in Tyler's Charles City County, and the prospect of his own slaves murdering him and his family in the dead of night seemed no mere phantom. Virginia's governor called out the state militia. Armed patrols were organized. Tyler joined the "Silver Greys," men too old to take to the field but who could still protect themselves and their neighbors. "Virginia is arming to the teeth," Tyler wrote his son Robert two months after Brown's assault. "More than fifty thousand stand of arms [are] already distributed, and the demand for more daily increasing. . . . But one sentiment pervades the country: security in the Union, or separation." Although the feared slave uprisings never occurred, life at Sherwood Forest never regained its old serenity. Tyler still believed that "after all, good may come out of evil," but, if the past was any guide, this was a vain hope.[14]

As the nation slid toward civil war in 1860, Tyler watched helplessly. National politics had become completely polarized—torn, it seemed, between the "slave power" and its Northern enemy, the Republican Party. It took the newly seated Thirty-sixth Congress two months to elect a speaker; talk of secession was in the air and legislators, feeling the need for protection, came armed to the House and Senate. Their skittishness was not irrational: in 1856, South Carolina congressman Preston Brooks beat Massachusetts senator Charles Sumner senseless with his gold-tipped gutta-percha cane; Sumner survived but was unable to return to the Senate for three years. In April 1860, the Democratic Party met in Charleston to select its presidential nominee but the result was bedlam. After losing a fight over a platform position that would have bound the federal government to protect slavery in the territories, angry Southern delegates stormed out. South Carolina's William Preston cried: "Slavery is our King; slavery is our Truth; slavery is our Divine Right." The Southerners cheered. When those who remained failed to produce a winner after fifty-seven ballots, the party decided to try again six weeks later in Baltimore. That convention managed to nominate Stephen Douglas, but again Southerners defected. They held their own convention and selected Kentucky's John C. Breckinridge, the vice president under President James Buchanan, to lead them. His platform called for the continued expansion of slavery in the territories and the acquisition of Cuba, where a new generation of slaves would flourish.[15]

Tyler thought the Southern walkout stupid and self-defeating. In unity there was strength; he believed they should have instead remained to throw their support behind a Northerner with Southern sympathies. (The South, in Tyler's opinion, would never again have one of its own in the White House. "I am the last of the Virginia Presidents," he said mournfully, in 1858.) Nevertheless, Tyler backed Breckinridge's candidacy, the South, and slavery. Adding to the electoral confusion was the Constitutional Union Party, consisting of old Whigs with vague principles, whose nominee, Tennessee's John Bell, called "for the Union, the Constitution, and the enforcement of the laws," whatever that meant. Tyler hoped that with all these contestants none would receive a majority and the outcome would be decided in the House, where the South might have a better chance to defeat Abraham Lincoln, the "Black Republican." That was not to be. The election results revealed "a nation breaking in two." Lincoln won the election with the Northern states plus Oregon and California, rich in electoral votes, while Breckinridge took the cotton states, Douglas secured the moderate Democrats in the Midwest and elsewhere, and Bell garnered the pro-Union Southerners in Kentucky, Tennessee, western Virginia, North Carolina, and Maryland.[16]

. . .

"We have fallen on evil times," Tyler noted after Lincoln's victory. "Madness rules the hour, and statesmanship . . . gives place to a miserable demagogism which leads to inevitable destruction." While the Republicans had rejected their more anti-Southern front-runner, New York governor William H. Seward, in favor of the moderate Lincoln, the president-elect would not permit slavery to grow beyond where it existed, and that, for Tyler, was the gravest danger. Virginia, Tyler wrote a friend, "will never consent to have her blacks cribbed and confined within proscribed and specified limits—and thus be involved in the consequences of a war of the races in some 20 or 30 years. She must have expansion, and if she cannot obtain for herself and her sisters that expansion in the Union, she may sooner or later look to Mexico, the West India Islands, and Central America as the ultimate reservations of the African race." While fearing for the South's future—he told his neighbors to sell their slaves or take them into the deep South—Tyler was not yet ready to abandon the Union.[17]

Others were. South Carolina radicals led the way in December 1860, and by early 1861, six more Southern states—Mississippi, Florida, Alabama, Georgia, Louisiana, and Tyler's beloved Texas—prepared to secede and join South Carolina in the Confederate States of America. It would be "a civilization that has never been equaled or surpassed," said South Carolina's Robert Barnwell Rhett, "a civilization teeming with orators, poets, philosophers, statesmen and historians equal to those of Greece and Rome."

At Sherwood Forest, Tyler searched desperately for a way to prevent the dissolution of the Union. He called for a peace conference to be held in Washington, D.C. At first, he proposed a group representing a dozen border states, half slave, half free. "They are the most interested in keeping the peace, and if they cannot come to an understanding, then the political union is gone," he noted in December 1860. If secession did occur, he hoped the South would be allowed to leave peacefully. They could revise the old Constitution to give the South the security it required and then invite the other states "to enter our Union with the old flag flying over one and all." The other alternative—war—was "too horrible and revolting" to contemplate.[18]

The Virginia legislature endorsed Tyler's plan for a peace convention but asked all the states, not simply the ones on the Missouri Compromise border, to send commissioners to the capital. The legislature also appointed Tyler as one of the state's commissioners— formally instructed to make "every effort in his power to effect a reconciliation"—while at the same time asking him to meet with President Buchanan to see if peace was still possible.

Physically, Tyler was not up to these tasks. He was seventy years old and suffering from a host of ailments—chronic bronchitis, especially in the winter months, frequent dysentery in summer, and his usual, but now more debilitating, intestinal problems, for which he took "heavy doses" of mercury laced with chalk. He had a low opinion of physicians and preferred to treat himself with quinine, "spiked with a jigger of whisky," and calomel, which probably worsened his conditions. Yet, despite these ills, he was determined to go to Washington. Like Lincoln, Tyler was afflicted by an ambition "that knew no rest." Preventing civil war would certainly earn him a place among the Virginia dynasty of presidents, perhaps making him the greatest of all. In this, Julia encouraged him. "The seceding States on hearing that he is conferring with Mr. Buchanan will stay . . . their proceedings out of respect for him," Julia confidently believed. "If the Northern States will only follow up this measure in a conceding Union, peace will be insured." She too would go to Washington; the nation might be on the brink of civil war, but it was also the social season.[19]

Tyler arrived on January 23, 1861, to find the city beset by rumors. "A widespread and powerful conspiracy" was afoot to seize the Capitol, many believed, while others expected Southern troops to appear at any moment. Reality was equally troubling: in South Carolina, state militias seized the federal arsenal in the capital and troops occupied Fort Moultrie and Castle Pinckney; when President Buchanan sent the *Star of the West* with troops and supplies to Fort Sumter, South Carolina's guns fired at it and the ship fled. If another attempt was made to relieve the fort, it was expected that armed conflict and civil war would result. Little time remained to prevent cataclysm, so, after taking a suite at Brown's Hotel, Tyler immediately contacted Buchanan, who agreed to meet with the former president the next morning at ten o'clock.[20]

Tyler had known the president for two decades and had earlier offered to appoint him to the Supreme Court. The nation would have been better served if Buchanan had taken that post, since it likely would have prevented him from becoming president, a job for which he was totally unsuited. Although their ninety-minute meeting was "warm and cordial," it was clear to Tyler that Buchanan was merely biding his time until he could leave the White House. "His policy," Tyler noted, "is obviously to throw all responsibility off of his shoulders." Buchanan complained that "the South had not treated him properly," seizing arsenals and forts, which he called "acts of useless bravado." Tyler urged the president to remain calm; such actions were only irritants, which would be forgotten once unity was restored. Buchanan agreed to ask Congress to avoid hostilities but told Tyler that "the entire . . . subject of war or peace" was up to that body. Tyler reminded Buchanan that he, as commander in chief, must do everything possible to avoid provoking the South and offered to help draft the president's message to Congress. Tyler left feeling that for the time being war was not imminent.[21]

His confidence was badly shaken the next day when, after approving Buchanan's message to Congress, Tyler learned that the steamship *Brooklyn*, with troops aboard, had set sail for Charleston. A "startled" Tyler searched the government for an explanation. Attorney General Edwin M. Stanton knew nothing of such a mission, while Secretary of State Jeremiah S. Black thought the *Brooklyn* was on the high seas, but had no idea where it was headed. Tyler scrawled a note to Buchanan and asked the attorney general to deliver it promptly. Stanton went directly to the White House but was unable to see the president, so left Tyler's message with a Buchanan "servant." At eleven fifteen that night, Tyler was awakened by a messenger carrying the president's reply: the *Brooklyn* "had gone on an errand of 'mercy and relief' " to Florida and "was not destined for South Carolina." Tyler slept easy that night and the following morning sent the good news to his colleagues in Charleston.[22]

Buchanan kept his promise. On Monday, January 28, he sent a special message to Congress asking it "to abstain from hostile measures." Tyler listened as it was read aloud and was pleased with the role he had played in its creation. But he was disappointed when both the Senate and the House treated Virginia's resolutions "with brutal indifference," refusing to refer them to committee or even have them printed, an "ordinary courtesy." And as Tyler was about to leave the capital, another disturbing event occurred—a newspaper story reported that the federal fort in Virginia had pointed its cannons inland at the commonwealth's citizens. Tyler dashed off another note to the president. "When Virginia is making every possible effort to redeem and save the Union," he said, "it is seemingly ungenerous to have cannon leveled at her bosom." Buchanan replied just as quickly, expressing ignorance of the fort's situation but pledging to look into it. Tyler's first mission to Washington had been mostly successful—he had helped stamp out rumors that might have led to serious violence and felt that Buchanan would do nothing to upset the status quo— but Congress's rejection of Virginia's plea for peace was deeply disturbing and suggested that the legislators would also ignore the peace convention, which was scheduled to open in less than one week.[23]

· · ·

When Tyler returned to Washington on February 3, the crisis had worsened. South Carolina was demanding the surrender of Fort

Sumter and Buchanan appeared unwilling or unable to act. General Winfield Scott urged the president to send warships to protect the fort and Buchanan agreed, then changed his mind, afraid of the consequences. He later informed South Carolina that without a congressional authorization he had no power to evacuate the fort, a response that the firebrands in Charleston called "highly insulting." Tyler suddenly became "the great center of attraction," Julia noted, mobbed by frantic people who expected him "to save the Union." However, some delegates were distinctly "unsympathetic," calling him a "traitor" and a "tottering ashen ruin," more hated than any man "who ever occupied the presidential chair." As in the old days, Tyler was poised between an earthquake and a tornado.[24]

When the peace convention met on February 5, he was quickly and unanimously elected its president. If they could achieve "the great work of reconciliation," Tyler told them, their names would be "enrolled in the Capitol, to be repeated by future generations with grateful applause. . . . You have to snatch from ruin a great and glorious Confederation; to preserve the Government and to renew and invigorate the Constitution. I confess myself ambitious of sharing in the glory of accomplishing this grand and magnificent result." Greeted by thunderous applause, his extemporaneous address was "one of the most affecting and eloquent efforts ever spoken in this country," wrote the *Evening Star*. Some reporters were surprised to find Tyler so "keen and well preserved" and were impressed by his vigorous delivery. "Who would have thought that the old man has so much blood in him," mused the editor of the *Examiner*. Tyler, gazing on the crowd, must have recalled his tragic and tumultuous past; among the 132 delegates was Charles Wickliffe, his postmaster general and one of the few friends to attend his wedding to Julia; Francis Granger and Thomas Ewing, members of his inherited cabinet who resigned in protest that memorable Saturday twenty years before; Robert Stockton, the captain of the USS *Princeton* who had since been elected a U.S. senator from New Jersey. In all, it was one of the most distinguished groups of public servants ever collected in one place. Tyler compared it to "our god-like [founding] fathers": besides a former U.S. president, there were ex-governors, senators, congressmen, ambassadors, Supreme Court justices, and cabinet secretaries. But too many were old and infirm—one died during the proceedings—and of the twenty-one states represented, only seven were in the South.[25]

The delegates' task was to draft a proposed constitutional amendment that would be acceptable to this divided body, Congress, and the four-fifths of the states needed for ratification—an improbable and difficult goal. While the resolutions committee set to work, President Buchanan called Tyler to the White House to again discuss the crisis in South Carolina. Tyler urged the president to evacuate Fort Sumter: it was indefensible and not worth a civil war. Buchanan refused. Instead he asked Tyler to send a message to the Palmetto State's angry governor, Francis Pickens, assuring him of the government's peaceful intentions. He did, and a few days later he learned that the governor, an old suitor of Julia's, had "calmed" down. Buchanan was so grateful that he honored Tyler by visiting him at Brown's Hotel, thanking him for his service to the country. "It is the first visit he has paid since being the nation's chief," the societally conscious Julia wrote her mother.[26]

The peace convention, however, was not progressing well. On February 9, six more Deep South states seceded. The convention's delegates could not reach a solution acceptable to Tyler and his fellow Southerners, let alone to Congress and the states. Tempers grew short and delegates exchanged threats. On at least one occasion, men almost came to blows. Tyler interceded. "Order," he yelled. "Shame upon the delegate who would dishonor this conference with violence."[27]

When Tyler realized that the final version of the proposed amendment would not allow slavery to grow in Latin America and the West Indies, he joined the seceding radicals. He now simply hoped to persuade the border states "and perhaps New Jersey" to become part of the new confederacy and thereby create a strong enough military force to deter incoming President Lincoln's government from choosing war—what biographer Robert Seager called "peace-through-secession-and-balance-of-power." On February 26, however, Tyler was persuaded that Lincoln did, in fact, want war. During a heated meeting, Lincoln insisted that soon he would take the oath to preserve, protect, and defend the Constitution. "The Constitution will not be preserved and defended until it is enforced and obeyed in every part of every one of the United States," he told peace commissioners. "It must be so respected, obeyed, enforced and defended." That was too much for some of the assembled Southerners, who quickly left the room. Tyler remained long enough to hear Lincoln remark, "In a choice of evils, war may not always be the worst."[28]

Three days later, Tyler joined the most radical Southerners to vote against the peace convention's amendment. It was approved by a majority of delegates and delivered to Congress, which ignored it. On February 28, he was back in Richmond, where, from the steps of the Exchange Hotel, he attacked the "Old Gentlemen's Conference" and forcefully urged Virginia to secede from the Union. But Tyler's words did not move the Old Dominion into the Confederacy. A swift series of events later that spring caused that misfortune: President Lincoln's inauguration on March 4; South Carolina's takeover of Fort Sumter on April 12; and Lincoln's call for seventy-five thousand volunteers to put down the insurrection on April 16. On the eve of Virginia's vote, Tyler wrote Julia: "The prospects now are that we shall have a war and a trying one. The battle at Charleston has aroused the whole North. I fear that . . . they will break upon the South with an immense force. . . . Submission or resistance is only left us. My hope is that the Border States will follow speedily our lead. If so, all will be safe. . . . These are dark times, dearest, and I think only of you and our little ones. . . . I shall vote secession."

On the afternoon of April 17, John Tyler joined eighty-seven other delegates to the Virginia state convention to approve an ordinance of secession and, in so doing, became the first president to betray the country he spent his life serving. Later that afternoon, Tyler and his friend Henry Wise celebrated Virginia's decision at

Richmond's Metropolitan Hall. To the crowd of happy rebels there assembled, Tyler spoke of America's first revolution and prayed that "Divine Providence would again crown our efforts with similar success."[29]

. . .

Although too old to join the fight, Tyler vigorously supported the South. He helped Virginia win admission to the Confederate States of America, oversaw the transfer of the Confederacy's capital from Montgomery, Alabama, to Richmond, and served in its provisional congress. Nor did his age and status prevent him from feeling the conflict's terrible impact. The war tore apart the Tyler-Gardiner family. Juliana Gardiner became a Copperhead—a staunch New York supporter of the Confederacy—but her son David remained a devoted Unionist, which enraged both her and Julia. "I think D. has been bitten by the rabid tone of those around him and the press," she wrote her mother in May. "I am utterly ashamed of the state in which I was born, and its people. All soul and magnanimity have departed from them." David Gardiner received a cool reception whenever he and his wife visited his mother. Robert Tyler, a struggling lawyer in Philadelphia when the war came, narrowly escaped lynching because of his Confederate sympathies; he, like his father before him, was burned in effigy. Eventually, Robert and Priscilla made their way safely to Richmond, where Robert found a job with the Confederate Treasury. John Jr. was commissioned a major in the Confederate army and Tazewell served as a surgeon. Three Tyler grandsons fought for the Confederacy, and young William Griffin Waller, the son of Elizabeth Tyler and William Waller, whose song saved John Tyler's life aboard the *Princeton*, was killed in action.[30]

In the fall of 1861, Tyler again sought elective office, running and decisively defeating "two of the ablest and most popular men in . . . Richmond" to win a seat in the Confederate House of Representatives. After the Christmas holidays, he packed his bags and rode to Richmond to begin his second career in Southern politics. Julia was scheduled to join him after visiting friends nearby, but she canceled

these plans after a terrible nightmare awakened her on the night of
January 9. She dreamed that her husband was seriously ill and, gathering her infant daughter Pearl, she rushed to the Exchange Hotel,
arriving late the following evening to find Congressman-elect Tyler
alive and well and amused to hear of Julia's tale of his premature demise.[31]

But on Sunday morning, Tyler awoke feeling ill. He became
nauseous, felt dizzy, and vomited. Since such symptoms were not
unusual given his intestinal problems, Tyler ignored them and,
telling Julia that he had a "chill," he went downstairs for a cup of
tea. That seemed to help, but as he rose to leave, he collapsed and
lost consciousness for a few minutes. When he came to, he found
himself lying on a couch in the hotel parlor surrounded by concerned employees. Again dismissing the episode, he got to his feet
and managed to return to his room. Julia, alarmed by his appearance, called for a doctor. After examining his patient, Dr. William
Peachy concluded that he was suffering from "a bilious attack,
united with bronchitis."[32]

During the next week, Tyler rested in his room and, despite frequent headaches and a bad cough, he met with friends and fellow
politicians to discuss the formation of the new Confederate Congress. Dr. Peachy gave him morphine, which helped him to sleep,
and Robert decided to stay with his father until he was better. As
the weekend approached, Peachy "insisted" that the Tylers return
to Sherwood Forest so that the busy legislator could "have perfect
quiet for a few days." But late Friday night, January 17, he awoke
"suddenly with a feeling of suffocation," and his gasping alarmed
his wife and son. Robert ran for the doctor, baby Pearl began to cry,
and Julia tried to care for both her husband and her daughter. "Poor
little thing," Tyler said, "how I disturb her." A Dr. Brown appeared
and urged Tyler to sip some brandy and then tried to apply mus-
tard plasters to his chest, which Tyler resisted, saying: "Doctor, I
think you are mistaken." It was almost 12:15 a.m. on January 18
when Dr. Peachy arrived. Tyler was slowly losing consciousness but
remarked, "Doctor, I am going."

"I hope not, Sir," Peachy replied.

"Perhaps it is best." Then, as Julia later recalled, "he looked forward with a radiant expression, as if he saw something to surprise and please, and then, as if falling asleep, was gone." The fainting spell, the headaches, and the breathing problems suggest that the cause of his death was a stroke. "The bed on which he died was exactly like the one I saw him upon in my dream and unlike any of our own," Julia observed.[33]

There was no White House funeral for John Tyler; no flags flew at half-staff at the Capitol or anywhere in the Northern states; no eulogies were lavished in the House or Senate, where he once served. The Lincoln government took no formal notice of his death, and there were few public obituaries. The *New York Times* noted that Tyler "added a new term to our political vocabulary . . . [the] infamous appellation of traitor." He died "amid the ruins of his native state," the *Times* concluded. "He himself was one of the architects of its ruin; and beneath that melancholy wreck his name will be buried."[34]

The former president of the United States received a Southern farewell a few days after his death. Tyler's open coffin, draped by the Confederate flag, lay in state in Richmond's Hall of Congress from Sunday until Tuesday, January 21. Thousands, "wearing badges of mourning," entered the hall for one "last look at his well-known features." At noon on Tuesday, the coffin was carried to the waiting hearse, which was driven to St. Paul's Episcopal Church. There, sixteen pallbearers—including some from the new Confederate states, but not Texas—carried the coffin into a church filled to overflowing. Joining the Tyler family were a host of dignitaries: Jefferson Davis, president of the Confederate States of America, accompanied by his vice president and cabinet, and the governor of Virginia. Members of the Confederate Congress and both houses of the Virginia state legislature attended. A choir sang. Then the Right Reverend Bishop Johns delivered the funeral service. Tyler, Bishop Johns said, "had left behind him a rich and pure legacy, worthy to adorn the history of his country and to guide others by example."

Later, as a gentle rain fell, a procession of 150 carriages, stretching over a quarter of a mile, followed the hearse bearing John Tyler's body through streets "filled with spectators" to Richmond's Hollywood Cemetery. Buried there were two other famous sons of the Old Dominion, the eccentric John Randolph, who dueled with Henry Clay, and James Monroe, the last president of the revolutionary generation. Tyler's final resting place, near Monroe's, is on a knoll overlooking his beloved James River, whose waters nurtured his family for a century.

Honored by the South, condemned by the North, in death as in life Tyler remained a controversial figure.[35]

Epilogue

A Matter Very Near to My Heart

In the winter of 1946, accidental president Harry S. Truman took time away from dealing with postwar strikes and troubles with the Russians to research his family's history. His relatives had always told him that his great-grandmother's brother was the tenth president of the United States, John Tyler. He believed the tale and it seemed likely every time he passed George P. A. Healy's "fine" official portrait of Tyler, which hung in the White House. "The President's features look like our family," Truman thought. So Truman did his homework and discovered that his family was wrong. Their John Tyler was not the former president. But Truman was relieved, not disappointed. He was a history buff, and what he read about Tyler upset him. "No one can charge John Tyler with a lack of courage," he wrote a friend in 1955. "He resigned from the Senate because he did not agree with Andrew Jackson, but I can never forgive him for leaving his party to join the Whigs, or for leaving the Union in 1861." He also thought that Tyler was "unpopular," inept, and "didn't amount to a great deal." Truman eventually concluded that Tyler was "one of the presidents we could have done without."[1]

Such judgments would have bothered Tyler because he was very concerned about his place in history. It was, he said, "a matter very near to my heart." He felt personally connected to Washington, Jefferson, Madison, and Monroe and vigorously fought to belong to the Virginia dynasty of presidents. In retirement, he quickly answered his critics, who not only affected his future standing but, despite all his wounds, still hurt him personally. "Every slight, every misrepresentation of his motives, cut him deeply," wrote biographer Robert Seager. Julia Tyler was especially worried about her husband's status and asked Robert Tyler and brother Alexander Gardiner to watch for hostile articles in the Eastern press and bring them immediately to the former president's attention. Tyler answered nearly every one and often had his responses reprinted and distributed nationally. After his death, his children continued to promote his reputation. In 1885, son Lyon, soon to be president of the College of William and Mary, published a long and loving multivolume history of the family entitled *The Letters and Times of the Tylers*. It defended his father's administration against its critics, whom the family called "poor old fools." Lyon was still hard at work forty-four years later when he answered *Time* magazine's assertion that, compared to Abraham Lincoln, John Tyler was "historically a dwarf."[2]

So far, the "poor old fools" have won—when they've remembered him at all, most analysts have concluded that John Tyler *was* a historical dwarf. Clinton Rossiter, the distinguished political scientist, believed that American political history from 1836 to 1860 was "a dull void" with "one bright spot": James K. Polk. When journalist-turned-historian Nathan Miller wrote about the presidency, he skipped Tyler, because, Miller believed, he was one of those lost nineteenth-century presidents once famously described by Thomas Wolfe: "Their gravely vacant and bewhiskered faces mixed, melted, swam together in the sea-depth of the past, intangible, immeasurable, and unknowable."[3] Indeed, the last two full Tyler biographies were written in 1939 and 1960, and in the latter Tyler shared the stage with the colorful Gardiner family.

Nor has Tyler fared well in the many presidential polls taken in the last forty years. From 1948, when Arthur M. Schlesinger Sr. first asked historians to rate our chief executives, to a 2005 *Wall Street Journal* survey, Tyler has appeared near the bottom of every list. A 2007 *U.S. News & World Report* cover story on "America's Worst Presidents" placed Tyler sixth among the ten "most dismal Commanders in Chief." Adding insult to injury, Tyler's picture was on the magazine's red, white, and blue cover beside three other honorees—Richard Nixon, Herbert Hoover, and Ulysses S. Grant.[4]

Some historians have been more positive. Norma Lois Peterson called the Tyler presidency "flawed" but insisted that others, especially the arrogant and vindictive Henry Clay, must share the blame for Tyler's failures on the domestic front. His solid achievements, especially in foreign policy, have been overlooked and he often "demonstrated exemplary executive skill and common sense." William and Mary's Edward Crapol also concluded that Tyler "was a stronger and more effective president than generally remembered." But ultimately he considered Tyler "a tragic figure" in American history. Tyler's "self-inflicted" wound lay in a Republican philosophy that sought the extension and preservation of a slaveholding America, Crapol argued. When that vision collided with "a competing anti-slavery nationalism dedicated to free soil, free men and an end to slavery's expansion," Tyler found himself on the wrong side of history, left the Union, and died a traitor, his good deeds forever tainted by his final years.[5]

It is unlikely that Tyler's historical reputation will recover from his last acts. Nevertheless, they should not obscure the importance of his presidency. For good and ill, Tyler preserved and defended the office from those who wished to fundamentally change it. By boldly assuming the full powers and prerogatives of the presidency upon Harrison's death, he established what came to be known as the "Tyler Precedent," not only ensuring the orderly transfer of power in his time but, by making the office "independent of death," guaranteeing that future accidental presidents could govern with authority. Americans apparently approved Tyler's decisive action when, in 1967, they ratified the Twenty-fifth Amendment to the Constitution, guaranteeing that "In the case of the removal of the President from office or of his death or resignation, the Vice President shall become President."

Tyler also protected the presidency by rejecting Whig efforts to weaken it. Although he did not believe that the president was the tribune of the people, as did Jackson, the Roosevelts, Truman, and Lyndon Johnson, he did not want to see the presidency become subservient to Congress. He refused to commit himself to serving only one term, used the veto vigorously, and fought all attempts to limit presidential power. Tyler showed that even a weakened president, without congressional or party support or the personal charisma to win wide popular approval, could have a significant impact on events. As Tyler's own government collapsed around him, he (and until 1843 Secretary of State Daniel Webster) improved British-American relations through the Webster-Ashburton Treaty; opened relations with China through the Treaty of Wangxia; extended the Monroe Doctrine to cover Hawaii; and annexed Texas. Of course, the greatest legacy among them—Texas—aggravated the mounting sectional crisis and led eventually to the Civil War.

Tyler not only protected the presidency from emasculation, he expanded its powers in ways that were troubling. As Arthur M. Schlesinger Jr. and Edward Crapol have noted, Tyler helped to create an "Imperial Presidency." His use of the secret service contingency fund and foreign agents responsible only to the president; his refusal to automatically grant Congress access to records he believed should remain confidential; dispatching army and navy forces to protect Texas; and choosing congressional resolutions to annex foreign territory mark a significant and disturbing chapter in the history of the presidency. He developed new weapons that, when used by future embattled presidents, damaged both the office and the nation.[6]

Tyler's record also demonstrates the particular hazards that face accidental presidents. Those whose principles are at odds with their predecessor or political party—as was the case with Tyler and Andrew Johnson—encountered difficulties that prevented them from winning a second term in the White House. Those who carried out or even broadened their fallen chief's policies—like Truman and Lyndon Johnson—had more successful presidencies and won power in their own right. Tyler came to power committed to a political ideology at odds with his party's leaders. When he stuck doggedly to it, there was chaos; when he abandoned it, he achieved his goals, good and bad. "[D]octrinaire adherence to an ideology, or a stiff-backed presidential personality . . . have been detriments to sensible, innovative leadership," historian Robert Dallek noted.[7] In short, pragmatists, not ideologues, make better presidents, as the best chief executives—Lincoln and FDR—realized. Similarly, Tyler's belief that he was heir to the Virginia dynasty drove him to act recklessly in pursuit of annexing Texas. Determined not to leave the White House "ignominiously nor soon be forgotten," he helped unleash furies that nearly destroyed his country and tarnished his own reputation. Those presidents who feel compelled to fulfill a familial or spiritual agenda often court disaster.

The mild-mannered gentleman from Virginia, scorned by his contemporaries, neglected by today's historians, and forgotten by his countrymen, deserves to be remembered and reexamined. There is much to be learned from his tumultuous presidency.

Notes

PROLOGUE: THE INSTRUMENT OF A NEW TEST

1. Tyler, vol. 1, pp. 11–12; Stathis, p. 225.
2. Quoted in Cleaves, p. 335.
3. Stathis, p. 226; Kunhardt, p. 21; Norma Peterson, p. 28; Seager, *Tyler Too*, p. 146; Marx, p. 131; Bumgarner, pp. 60–62; Nevins, *Hone*, pp. 535, 537; Cleaves, p. 342.
4. Schlesinger, *Cycles*, pp. 345–46; Widmer, pp. 119–20.
5. Crapol, p. 8.
6. Dinnerstein, p. 447; Stathis, p. 225; Shelley, p. 339; Crapol, pp. 8–9, Norma Peterson, pp. 45, 47.
7. Seager, *Tyler Too*, p. 148; Crapol, pp. 9–10; Chitwood, p. 203.
8. Seager, *Tyler Too*, p. 575, n. 18; Adams is quoted in Schlesinger, *Cycles*, p. 344.
9. Kunhardt, p. 211; Norma Peterson, pp. 66–67; Schlesinger, *Imperial Presidency*, p. 344; Young, pp. 45–47; Silva, pp. 14–23.
10. Seager, *Tyler Too*, p. 149.
11. Ibid., pp. 149–50; Tyler, vol. 3, p. 20.

1: THE HIGH ROAD TO FAME

1. Tyler, vol. 1, pp. 229–30; Chitwood, pp. 8–10, 19–20; Monroe, *Republican Vision*, p. 16.
2. Tyler, vol. 1, pp. 55–56; Chitwood, pp. 6–10, 19–20; Monroe, *Republican Vision*, p. 16; Seager, *Tyler Too*, p. 51.
3. Tyler, vol. 1, p. 54.
4. Seager, *Tyler Too*, pp. 48, 50–51; on Judge Tyler as father see Leahy, pp. 325–30, 337.

5. Dunn, pp. 3–5; Tyler, vol. 1, p. 194.
6. Monroe, *Republican Vision*, pp. 8–14; Dunn, pp. 34–35.
7. Leahy, p. 334; Seager, *Tyler Too*, pp. 48, 50; Chitwood, pp. 16–17; Crapol, p. 31; Marx, p. 134; Israel, p. 106.
8. Leahy, p. 328; Israel, p. 112.
9. Crapol, pp. 3, 33.
10. Israel, pp. 112–13.
11. Leahy, p. 325; Seager, *Tyler Too*, p. 50; Chitwood, p. 20; Monroe, *Republican Vision*, p. 16; Tyler, vol. 1, pp. 204, 228.
12. Seager, *Tyler Too*, p. 54; Chitwood, p. 21; Israel, p. 114; Tyler, vol. 1, p. 272.
13. Tyler, vol. 1, p. 274; Monroe, *Republican Vision*, pp. 16–17; Seager, *Tyler Too*, pp. 55–56; Chitwood, pp. 27–28.
14. Seager, *Tyler Too*, pp. 56–57; Chitwood, pp. 24–25; Tyler, vol. 1, pp. 276–77.
15. Tyler, vol. 1, pp. 267–69.
16. Ibid., pp. 276–77; Seager, *Tyler Too*, p. 58.
17. Hickey, p. 154.
18. Seager, *Tyler Too*, pp. 58–59; Tyler, vol. 1, pp. 277–79; Chitwood, pp. 29–30.
19. Widmer, p. 54; Chitwood, p. 41; Seager, *Tyler Too*, p. 60.
20. Tyler, vol. 1, pp. 289–91; Seager, *Tyler Too*, p. 60; Remini, *Clay*, pp. 143–46.
21. Remini, *Clay*, pp. 135–43; Tyler, vol. 1, p. 288.
22. Tyler, vol. 1, p. 294; Chitwood, pp. 32–34, emphasis in original; Seager, *Tyler Too*, p. 61.
23. Wilentz, *Rise*, pp. 205–17; Dangerfield, pp. 179–89; Monroe, *Republican Vision*, pp. 29–30.
24. Tyler, vol. 1, pp. 302–3; Monroe, *Republican Vision*, pp. 28–30; Seager, *Tyler Too*, p. 64.
25. Crapol, p. 39; Monroe, *Republican Vision*, pp. 30–33; Seager, *Tyler Too*, pp. 64–65; Dangerfield, pp. 189–96; Tyler, vol. 1, p. 499; Dunn, p. 122.
26. Agar, pp. 203–4; Remini, *Clay*, pp. 177–78, 183; Seager, *Tyler Too*, p. 69.
27. Crapol, pp. 58–63; Seager, *Tyler Too*, pp. 53, 68–69; Tyler, vol. 1, p. 313.
28. Tyler, vol. 1, pp. 317–24; Monroe, *Republican Vision*, pp. 40–45; Chitwood, pp. 49–50.
29. Tyler, vol. 1, p. 335; Seager, *Tyler Too*, pp. 71–72.
30. Tyler, vol. 1, p. 316; Marx, p. 134.
31. Marx, p. 134; Bumgarner, p. 65.
32. Leahy, pp. 336–37; Tyler, vol. 1, pp. 316–17, 340.
33. Tyler, vol. 1, p. 337.

2: THE SENTINEL

1. Leahy, pp. 336–39.
2. Seager, *Tyler Too*, p. 73.
3. Leahy, p. 339; Dunn, pp. 15–29.
4. Tyler, vol. 1, pp. 341–44; Chitwood, pp. 61–64, 67–69.
5. Agar, p. 109; Chitwood, pp. 78, 82; Remini, *Clay*, p. 78.
6. Remini, *Clay*, pp. 292–95; Tyler, vol.1, p. 362.
7. Crapol, pp. 62–63; Chitwood, pp. 85–86.
8. Wilentz, *Jackson*, pp. 14–17; Hofstadter, pp. 59–60.
9. Seager, *Tyler Too*, p. 68; Risjord, pp. 188–89; Monroe, *Republican Vision*, pp. 181–82.
10. Burns, p. 319; Hofstadter, pp. 60–64; Wilentz, *Jackson*, pp. 35–43; Seager, *Tyler Too*, p. 68.
11. Wilentz, *Jackson*, pp. 45–47.
12. Ibid., pp. 46–49; Wilentz, *Rise*, pp. 254–57.
13. Seager, *Tyler Too*, pp. 62, 74–75.
14. Tyler, vol. 1, p. 377; Seager, *Tyler Too*, p. 79; Wilentz, *Jackson*, pp. 50–51.
15. Chitwood, pp. 87–88.
16. Tyler, vol. 1, pp. 375, 378; Risjord, pp. 268–69; Seager, *Tyler Too*, pp. 80–81.
17. Seager, *Tyler Too*, p. 82; Remini, *Election*, pp. 151–53; Remini, *Jackson: Freedom*, pp. 133–34.
18. Remini, *Adams*, p. 127; Remini, *Election*, pp. 187–91; Smith, pp. 11–13.
19. Tyler, vol. 1, p. 412; Chitwood, pp. 99–100; Wilentz, *Jackson*, pp. 71–73; Abell, p. 99; Remini, *Clay*, pp. 396–98; Monroe, *Republican Vision*, pp. 53–54; Seager, *Tyler Too*, pp. 91–92.
20. Remini, *Jackson: Freedom*, p. 345.
21. Ibid., pp. 342–43; Remini, *Clay*, p. 398; Seager, *Tyler Too*, p. 88.
22. Wilentz, *Jackson*, p. 81; Chitwood, pp. 124–25; Smith, pp. 48, 59; Remini, *Clay*, p. 365.
23. Wilentz, *Jackson*, pp. 82–83; Remini, *Clay*, pp. 366–70.
24. Tyler, vol. 1, pp. 428–29, 439; Seager, *Tyler Too*, pp. 89–90; Wilentz, *Jackson*, pp. 86–87; Remini, *Jackson: Freedom*, pp. 389–92; Remini, *Clay*, pp. 402–11.
25. Hofstadter, p. 73; Merrill Peterson, p. 256.
26. Hofstadter, pp. 71–72; Monroe, *Republican Vision*, p. 5; Remini, *Clay*, pp. 413–14; Wilentz, *Jackson*, pp. 93–94; Van Deusen, p. 72.
27. Wilentz, *Jackson*, pp. 94–97; Latner, p. 118; Monroe, *Republican Vision*, pp. 58–59; Remini, *Clay*, p. 414; Remini, *Jackson: Democracy*, pp. 17–23; Van Deusen, pp. 74–75; Tyler, vol. 1, pp. 444–45.

28. Chitwood, pp. 118–19.
29. Remini, *Clay*, pp. 415–18.
30. Ibid., p. 418; Brands, pp. 476–77, 481; Tyler, vol. 1, p. 446.
31. Tyler, vol. 1, p. 448; Seager, *Tyler Too*, pp. 85, 92–93; Remini, *Jackson: Democracy*, pp. 3, 36.
32. Tyler, vol. 1, pp. 456–57; Seager, *Tyler Too*, pp. 93–94.
33. Monroe, *Republican Vision*, pp. 64–65; Remini, *Jackson: Democracy*, p. 36.
34. Tyler, vol. 1, pp. 453–55.
35. Remini, *Clay*, pp. 425–26; Remini, *Jackson: Democracy*, p. 35.
36. Seager, *Tyler Too*, p. 95; Chitwood, p. 115; Remini, *Jackson: Democracy*, p. 39.
37. Tyler, vol. 1, p. 462.
38. Latner, p. 19; Brands, p. 498.
39. Seager, *Tyler Too*, pp. 98–99; Tyler, vol. 1, pp. 490–91; Chitwood, pp. 125–26.
40. Monroe, *Republican Vision*, pp. 70–72; Seager, *Tyler Too*, pp. 98–100.
41. Remini, *Jackson: Democracy*, p. 151; Wilentz, *Rise*, p. 344; Seager, *Tyler Too*, p. 101.
42. Remini, *Jackson: Democracy*, pp. 151–60; Remini, *Clay*, pp. 464, 467.
43. Chitwood, pp. 133–35; Seager, *Tyler Too*, pp. 110–11.
44. Seager, *Tyler Too*, p. 112.
45. Ibid., pp. 108, 114.
46. Tyler, vol. 1, pp. 534–36; Seager, *Tyler Too*, pp. 114–15, 131; Chitwood, pp. 132, 162.

3: TIPPECANOE AND TYLER TOO

1. Remini, *Clay*, p. 495.
2. Seager, *Tyler Too*, pp. 115–17; Holt, p. 39; Remini, *Jackson: Democracy*, pp. 136–41.
3. Remini, *Clay*, pp. 458–66, 473.
4. Ibid., pp. 490–93; Seager, *Tyler Too*, pp. 120–22.
5. Smith, pp. 344–45; Widmer, p. 96.
6. Burns, pp. 344–45; Curtis, p. 134.
7. Remini, *Clay*, pp. 505–6.
8. Chitwood, pp. 157–59.
9. Tyler, vol. 1, p. 591; Chitwood, p. 162, n. 12; Remini, *Clay*, pp. 530, 591–92; Seager, *Tyler Too*, p. 131.
10. Remini, *Clay*, pp. 548–50; Norma Peterson, p. 291; Holt, pp. 101–5.
11. Chitwood, pp. 166–67; Remini, *Clay*, pp. 551–55; Gunderson, *Log-Cabin*, pp. 62–64, 68; Holt, p. 104; Seager, *Tyler Too*, pp. 134–35; Chitwood, pp. 167–72; Norma Peterson, p. 292; Wilentz, *Rise*,

p. 497; Nevins, *Hone*, p. 553; Tyler, vol. 1, p. 595. Lyon Gardiner Tyler, a dutiful son, argues that his father "was from the start the choice of a large majority of the convention," but the facts do not support this assertion.

12. Gunderson, *Log-Cabin*, p. 64; Abell, p. 175.
13. Tyler, vol. 1, pp. 618–19; Seager, *Tyler Too*, p. 135.
14. Gunderson, *Log-Cabin*, pp. 74, 141–42.
15. Chitwood, p. 178; Gunderson, *Log-Cabin*, p. 113.
16. Burns, pp. 419–20.
17. Seager, *Tyler Too*, pp. 135–36; Agar, pp. 286–87.
18. Chitwood, p. 186; Gunderson, *Log-Cabin*, p. 195.
19. Gunderson, *Log-Cabin*, pp. 196–98.
20. Ibid., pp. 196–97; Chitwood, pp. 188–92; Tyler, vol. 1, pp. 619–23.
21. Holt, pp. 106, 112–13; Gunderson, *Log-Cabin*, pp. 257–58.
22. Gunderson, *Log-Cabin*, p. 257; Seager, *Tyler Too*, p. 141; Chitwood, p. 196.
23. Cleaves, pp. 113–14; Remini, *Clay*, pp. 94, 274–75, 555.
24. Tyler, vol. 3, p. 87; Seager, *Tyler Too*, p. 143.
25. Tyler, vol. 3, p. 10.
26. Clay to Harrison, March 15, 1841, in Seager, *Tyler Too*, pp. 516–17; Remini, *Clay*, pp. 567–77; Cleaves, pp. 339–40; Seager, *Tyler Too*, p. 145.

4: AMID EARTHQUAKE AND TORNADO

1. Chitwood, p. 207.
2. Ibid., p. 203; Cleaves, pp. 342–43; Gunderson, *Log-Cabin*, p. 273; Seager, *Tyler Too*, p. 144.
3. "Inaugural Address," in Richardson, pp. 11–15.
4. Norma Peterson, p. 52; Stathis, pp. 229–30.
5. Clay to James F. Conover, April 9, 1841; Clay to Nathaniel Beverley Tucker, April 15, 1841; Clay to John Q. Adams, April 29, 1841, in Seager, *Papers*, pp. 518, 520, 524.
6. Tyler to Clay, April 30, 1841, in Seager, *Papers*, pp. 527–28; Remini, *Clay*, p. 581; Norma Peterson, p. 54.
7. Tyler, vol. 3, p. 19; Seager, *Tyler Too*, pp. 105–7.
8. Wead, pp. 339–40; Nevins, *Adams*, p. 543.
9. Anthony, pp. 131–32; Chitwood, p. 390; Seager, *Tyler Too*, pp. 178–79.
10. Coleman, p. 91; Seager, *Tyler Too*, pp. 174–75.
11. Chitwood, pp. 386–87; Seager, *Tyler Too*, p. 178.
12. Burns, p. 423; Remini, *Clay*, pp. 583–84.
13. Chitwood, p. 226.
14. Ibid., p. 225, n. 21.

15. Nevins, *Adams*, p. 528; Tyler, vol. 3, pp. 71–72; Chitwood, pp. 226, 231.
16. Nevins, *Hone*, pp. 542, 552–53; Chitwood, p. 227.
17. Coleman, p. 85; Remini, *Clay*, p. 591.
18. Merrill Peterson, pp. 311–12; Remini, *Clay*, pp. 595–96.
19. Malenson, p. 133; Remini, *Clay*, p. 591.
20. Remini, *Clay*, p. 591.
21. Wilentz, *Rise*, p. 525; Norma Peterson, pp. 77–79.
22. Wilentz, *Rise*, p. 525; Seager, *Tyler Too*, pp. 157–58; Lambert, pp. 40–41; Norma Peterson, p. 79.
23. Norma Peterson, p. 312.
24. Chitwood, pp. 250–51; Norma Peterson, p. 91.
25. Chitwood, pp. 272–73.
26. Seager, *Tyler Too*, p. 161; Morgan, p. 70; Tyler, vol. 2, pp. 121–22, n. 1, emphasis in original; Remini, *Clay*, pp. 597–98; Merrill Peterson, pp. 84, 312–13.
27. Tyler, vol. 2, p. 129; Holt, p. 138; Norma Peterson, pp. 83–84, 87–88.
28. Holt, p. 138; Norma Peterson, pp. 55, 89.
29. Norma Peterson, pp. 89–90; Seager, *Tyler Too*, p. 162.
30. Clay is quoted in Remini, *Clay*, pp. 598–99.
31. Merrill Peterson, p. 312; Remini, *Clay*, pp. 581, 597. See also Allan Nevins's criticism of Tyler in Nevins, *Hone*, p. 554; Kunhardt, p. 215.

5: ABUSED AS NEVER BEFORE

1. Chitwood, pp. 290–91.
2. Holt, pp. 139–140.
3. Chitwood, p. 293.
4. Remini, *Clay*, pp. 605, 607.
5. Tyler is quoted in Seager, *Tyler Too*, p. 169.
6. Nevins, *Hone*, p. 645; Chitwood, pp. 299–300, 301–2.
7. Seager, *Tyler Too*, pp. 168–69.
8. Anthony, p. 123; Tyler, vol. 2, p. 172; Chitwood, pp. 395–96.
9. Coleman, p. 99; Chitwood, pp. 395–96.
10. Burns, p. 446.
11. Jones, pp. 20–32.
12. Ibid., pp. 33–47; Burns, p. 447; Merk, *Fruits*, pp. 5–7; Chitwood, p. 308; Bailey, pp. 207–8.
13. Burns, p. 447; Jones, pp. 49–65; Merk, *Fruits*, p. 11.
14. Chitwood, p. 306, n. 3; Jones, pp. 69–86.
15. Crapol, pp. 97–104; Merrill Peterson, p. 324; Chitwood, p. 316.
16. Jones, pp. 96–98.
17. Crapol, p. 100; Nevins, *Hone*, p. 595.

18. Merk, *Fruits*, p. 13; Crapol, pp. 109–10; Norma Peterson, p. 121; Remini, *Webster*, pp. 538–41.

19. Banks and Raven-Hansen, p. 102; Crapol, pp. 107–10; Merk, *Fruits*, pp. 8–10, 176–220; Jones, p. 94; Remini, *Webster*, pp. 564, 568.

20. Crapol, p. 104.

21. Nevins, *Hone*, p. 594; Jones, p. 118; Nevins, *Adams*, pp. 540–41.

22. Chitwood, p. 310.

23. Tyler, vol. 3, p. 218; Crapol, p. 111; Chitwood, p. 311.

24. Chitwood, pp. 311–12.

25. Crapol, pp. 111–14.

26. Jones, p. 163.

27. Norma Peterson, p. 130; Merrill Peterson, p. 329; Jones, p. 165.

28. Nevins, *Hone*, pp. 562, 618–19; Norma Peterson, pp. 130–31; Jones, p. 168.

29. Norma Peterson, p. 130; Chitwood, p. 316.

30. Seager, *Tyler Too*, p. 210; Crapol, pp. 118–21.

31. Tyler, vol. 2, p. 358; Seager, *Tyler Too*, p. 211; Crapol, pp. 162–70.

32. Seager, *Tyler Too*, pp. 17–26, 35, 180, 195; Harris, pp. 164–65; Cawthorne, p. 77.

33. Anthony, p. 123; Seager, *Tyler Too*, pp. 36–39.

34. Seager, *Tyler Too*, pp. 180–84.

35. Anthony, pp. 123–24; Seager, *Tyler Too*, p. 193.

36. Anthony, p. 124.

37. Merrill Peterson, p. 334; Seager, *Tyler Too*, p. 209.

6: THE LUSTER

1. Ticknor in Merk, *Slavery*, pp. 268–71; Crapol, p. 210; Sibley, pp. xvii–xviii.

2. Bailey, p. 240.

3. Sibley, pp. 14–17; Bailey, pp. 241–42.

4. Bailey, pp. 242–43.

5. Sibley, p. 27; Freehling, p. 369.

6. Chitwood, p. 343; Crapol, pp. 177–78; Norma Peterson, pp. 176–78, 185.

7. Crapol, pp. 121, 184.

8. Tyler, vol. 2, p. 388; Norma Peterson, p. 183; Seager, *Tyler Too*, p. 213.

9. Seager, *Tyler Too*, p. 225; Nevins, *Hone*, pp. 620–21.

10. Nevins, *Hone*, pp. 620–21, 692–93; Crapol, pp. 184–85; Seager, *Tyler Too*, p. 235.

11. Crapol, p. 185; Henry Huggins to Alexander G. Abell, December 9, 1843, Abell correspondence, Syracuse University, at http://library.syr.edu/digital/guides/a/abell_ag.htm.

12. Crapol, pp. 181–82; Seager, *Tyler Too*, p. 215; Sibley, p. 34.
13. Norma Peterson, pp. 176–77; Sibley, p. 117.
14. Chitwood, p. 330; Coleman, p. 104; Crapol, pp. 186–87.
15. Nevins, *Hone*, p. 660; Coleman, p. 104.
16. Chitwood, pp. 322, 326–30; Crapol, p. 191.
17. Crapol, pp. 192–93.
18. Nevins, *Adams*, pp. 550–51.
19. Tyler, vol. 2, p. 387; Norma Peterson, p. 182.
20. Crapol, p. 195.
21. Crapol, p. 201; Merk, *Fruits*, pp. 33–43.
22. Tyler, vol. 2, p. 390; Seager, *Tyler Too*, pp. 203, 582, n. 61; Blackman, *Wild Rose*, p. 129.
23. Tyler, vol. 2, p. 391; Seager, *Tyler Too*, pp. 205–6.
24. Ann Blackman, "Fatal Cruise of the Princeton," *Navy History*, September 2005, at http://www.military.com/New Content/0,13190, NH_0905_Cruise-P1,00,html; Nevins, *Adams*, p. 567.
25. Blackman, "Fatal Cruise."
26. Tyler, vol. 2, p. 390; Seager, *Tyler Too*, pp. 207–8.
27. Merk, *Slavery*, p. 53; Seager, *Tyler Too*, pp. 216–17; Norma Peterson, pp. 203–5; Crapol, pp. 211–12.
28. Crapol, pp. 213, 217; Nevins, *Adams*, p. 569.

7: THE CAPTAIN'S BRIDE

1. Merk, *Slavery*, p. 68; Sibley, p. 45.
2. Merk, *Slavery*, pp. 57–60.
3. Nevins, *Hone*, pp. 701–2; Van Deusen, p. 182; Sellers in Israel, pp. 761–62.
4. Seigenthaler, p. 79.
5. Seager, *Tyler Too*, pp. 228–30; Sellers, pp. 765–75.
6. Nevins, *Hone*, p. 706; Nevins, *Adams*, p. 570.
7. Crapol, pp. 218–19.
8. Seager, *Tyler Too*, pp. 3–4, 6.
9. Boller, p. 82; Seager, *Tyler Too*, p. 207.
10. Ibid.
11. Seager, *Tyler Too*, p. 5; Nevins, *Hone*, pp. 707–8; Harris, p. 166.
12. Seager, *Tyler Too*, pp. 5–6.
13. Nevins, *Adams*, pp. 571–72; Seager, *Tyler Too*, pp. 14–15, 258.
14. Seager, *Tyler Too*, pp. 7–8.
15. Ibid., pp. 8–9; Harris, p. 166.
16. Seager, *Tyler Too*, p. 9.
17. Ibid., pp. 231–33.
18. Ibid., pp. 230–31; Norma Peterson, pp. 237–38.

19. Seager, *Tyler Too*, pp. 236–37; Norma Peterson, pp. 239–40; Keller, p. 107.
20. Holt, pp. 194–207; Sibley, p. 79.
21. Seager, *Tyler Too*, pp. 239–42.
22. Anthony, p. 129.
23. Ibid.; Harris, p. 168; Boller, p. 83; Crapol, p. 219.
24. Seager, *Tyler Too*, pp. 246–48, 258; Anthony, p. 131.
25. Seager, *Tyler Too*, p. 281; Nevins, *Hone*, pp. 725–26.
26. Seager, *Tyler Too*, p. 282; Norma Peterson, p. 256.
27. Norma Peterson, pp. 256–57.
28. Tyler, vol. 2, p. 369; Van Deusen, pp. 190–91; *Howe*, p. 699; Nevins, *Hone*, p. 727; Sibley, pp. 87–88.
29. Seager, *Tyler Too*, pp. 262–65; Anthony, pp. 132–33.
30. Tyler, vol. 2, p. 369; Seager, *Tyler Too*, p. 283.

8: NO REST

1. Chitwood, pp. 411, 420–21.
2. Ibid., pp. 421–23.
3. Seager, *Tyler Too*, pp. 334–39, 350, 358; Boller, p. 82.
4. Seager, *Tyler Too*, p. 344.
5. Ibid., pp. 312–31, 333.
6. Chitwood, pp. 423–24; Seager, *Tyler Too*, pp. 322–25.
7. Crapol, p. 227.
8. Seager, *Tyler Too*, pp. 331–32.
9. Widmer, pp. 153–57; McPherson, p. 69.
10. Burns, pp. 472–74.
11. Seager, *Tyler Too*, p. 395; Nevins, *Hone*, pp. 922–23.
12. Burns, p. 551.
13. Ibid., p. 590.
14. Seager, *Tyler Too*, pp. 428–32.
15. Burton, p. 50.
16. Agar, p. 401; Seager, *Tyler Too*, pp. 438–39; Burton, pp. 102, 103.
17. Seager, *Tyler Too*, p. 444; Crapol, p. 257.
18. Seager, *Tyler Too*, p. 449.
19. Bumgarner, p. 65; Seager, *Tyler Too*, p. 451.
20. Gunderson, *Old*, pp. 1, 7; Baker, pp. 138–39.
21. Tyler, vol. 2, pp. 587–89; Seager, *Tyler Too*, pp. 451–52.
22. Tyler, vol. 2, pp. 590–91.
23. Ibid., pp. 591–92.
24. Ibid., p. 597; Gunderson, *Old*, p. 10.
25. Gunderson, *Old*, pp. 9–13.
26. Seager, *Tyler Too*, p. 455.

27. Gunderson, *Old*, p. 70.
28. Ibid., pp. 458–59.
29. Crapol, p. 265.
30. Seager, *Tyler Too*, pp. 463–67.
31. Tyler, vol. 2, pp. 669–71; Seager, *Tyler Too*, pp. 469–70.
32. Tyler, vol. 2, p. 672; Seager, *Tyler Too*, p. 470.
33. Tyler, vol. 2, pp. 666–67; Seager, *Tyler Too*, p. 471.
34. *New York Times*, January 22, 1862; Crapol, p. 273.
35. Tyler, vol. 2, p. 684; Seager, *Tyler Too*, p. 472.

EPILOGUE: A MATTER VERY NEAR TO MY HEART

1. Healy, p. 59; Ferrell, pp. 82, 265.
2. Seager, *Tyler Too*, p. 552; "Tyler v. Lincoln," *Time* magazine online, at http://www.time.com/time/magazine/article/0,9171,731816-2,00.html; Monroe, "Lincoln the Dwarf."
3. Norma Peterson, p. 261; Miller, p. 12; Karabell, p. 4.
4. Riddings and McIver, pp. 67–71; Jay Tolson, "Ten Worst Presidents," pp. 41–53; Miller, p. 12.
5. Norma Peterson, pp. 261–72; Crapol, pp. 282–83.
6. Schlesinger, *Imperial Presidency*, pp. 39–41, 46–48, 334–35, 447; Crapol, pp. 279–81.
7. Dallek, p. 77.

M i l e s t o n e s

1840   Elected vice president of the United States under
        William Henry Harrison

1841   Sworn in as vice president of the United States on
        March 4
        President William Henry Harrison becomes first
        president to die in office, April 4
        Tyler sworn in as tenth president of the United
        States, April 6; issues "Inaugural Address"
        Convenes Special Session of Congress
        Vetoes legislation rechartering Second Bank of the
        United States submitted by Senator Henry Clay
        "Ruffians" attack White House, leading to creation of
        first White House police force
        Vetoes second BUS bill
        Forms new cabinet after Harrison-Tyler cabinet,
        except for Secretary of State Daniel Webster, resigns
        Expelled from Whig Party
        Rhode Island Dorr rebellion

1842   Vetoes tariff bill
        House committee considers impeaching Tyler
        Senate approves Treaty of Washington
        Tyler approves new tariff bill
        Letitia Christian Tyler becomes first presidential wife
        to die in the White House
        U.S. extends Monroe Doctrine, protecting the
        Hawaiian islands from European colonization, a
        policy that comes to be known as the Tyler Doctrine

1843   Courts Julia Gardiner
        Secretary of State Daniel Webster resigns and is
        succeeded by Abel P. Upshur
        Upshur begins negotiations for treaty annexing Texas

1844   The USS *Princeton*'s Peacemaker cannon explodes
        with Tyler on board; Secretary of State Upshur, the
        secretary of the navy, and others are killed

John C. Calhoun becomes secretary of state;
negotiations with Texans resumed

Treaty with Texas signed

Nominated for the presidency by the Democratic-
Republican Party

Marries twenty-four-year-old Julia Gardiner; their
union eventually produces seven children

U.S. and China sign Treaty of Wangxia

Withdraws from 1844 presidential contest

Democratic candidate James K. Polk elected president

Asks Congress to annex Texas through joint resolution

1845	Congress passes and Tyler signs resolution of Texas annexation
1846	Testifies before House Foreign Affairs Committee in defense of Secretary of State Daniel Webster's handling of Maine crisis
1846–48	U.S.-Mexican War
1850	Supports Compromise of 1850
1854	Supports Kansas-Nebraska Act
1856	"Bloody Kansas"
1859	John Brown attack on Harpers Ferry, Virginia
1860	Abraham Lincoln elected president
1861	Meets with outgoing president James Buchanan
	Elected president of a peace convention to help resolve sectional crisis
	Virginia secedes from the Union
	Elected to Confederate House of Representatives
1862	Dies January 18 in Richmond, Virginia, and buried in Hollywood Cemetery

Selected Bibliography

Most of John Tyler's personal papers were destroyed when Union forces invaded Virginia during the Civil War. What remains are principally collected in the John Tyler Papers housed at the Library of Congress and in the Gardiner-Tyler Papers at Yale University. Lyon Gardiner Tyler's three-volume history of his family, *The Letters and Times of the Tylers* (Richmond, Va.: Whittet & Shepperson, 1884, 1885, 1886), contains important family correspondence. The best source for the literature on Tyler and his times is *John Tyler: A Bibliography*, compiled by Harold D. Moser (Westport, Conn.: Greenwood Publishing Group, 2001).

Abell, Alexander Gordon. *Life of John Tyler.* New York: Harper and Brothers, 1844.

Agar, Herbert. *The Price of Union.* Boston: Houghton Mifflin, 1950.

Anthony, Carl Sferrazza. *First Ladies: The Saga of the Presidents' Wives and Their Power, 1789–1961.* New York: William Morrow, 1990.

Bailey, Thomas A. *A Diplomatic History of the American People.* Englewood Cliffs, N.J.: Prentice Hall, 1974.

Baker, Jean H. *James Buchanan.* New York: Times Books, 2004.

Banks, William C., and Peter Raven-Hansen. *National Security and the Power of the Purse.* New York: Oxford University Press, 1994.

Barker, Robert. *Dead Certain: The Presidency of George W. Bush.* New York: Free Press, 2007.

Blackman, Ann. *Wild Rose: The True Story of a Civil War Spy.* New York: Random House, 2006.

Boller, Paul F., Jr. *Presidential Wives: An Anecdotal History.* New York: Oxford University Press, 1998.

Brands, H. W. *Andrew Jackson: His Life and Times.* New York: Doubleday, 2005.

Bumgarner, John R. *The Health of the Presidents*. Jefferson, N.C.: McFarland, 2004.

Burns, James MacGregor. *The Vineyard of Liberty*. New York: Vintage, 1982.

Burton, Orville Vernon. *The Age of Lincoln*. New York: Hill and Wang, 2007.

Cawthorne, Nigel. *Sex Lives of the Presidents*. New York: St. Martin's Press, 1996.

Chitwood, Oliver Perry. *John Tyler: Champion of the Old South*. Newtown, Conn.: American Political Biography Press, 1990.

Cleaves, Freeman. *Old Tippecanoe: William Henry Harrison and His Time*. New York: Charles Scribner's Sons, 1939.

Coleman, Elizabeth Tyler. *Priscilla Cooper Tyler and the American Scene, 1816–1889*. Tuscaloosa: University of Alabama Press, 1955.

Crapol, Edward P. *John Tyler, The Accidental President*. Chapel Hill: University of North Carolina Press, 2006.

Curtis, James C. "Martin Van Buren." In Philip Kunhardt, Jr., Philip B. Kunhardt III, and Peter W. Kunhardt, eds. *The American President*. New York: Riverhead Books, 1999.

Dallek, Robert. *Hail to the Chief: The Making and Unmaking of American Presidents*. New York: Hyperion, 1996.

Dinnerstein, Leonard. "The Accession of John Tyler to the Presidency." *Virginia Magazine of History and Biography* 70 (October 1962), pp. 447–58.

Dunn, Susan. *Dominion of Memories: Jefferson, Madison, and the Decline of Virginia*. New York: Basic Books, 2007.

Ferrell, Robert, ed. *Off the Record: The Private Papers of Harry S. Truman*. New York: Harper & Row, 1980.

Freehling, William W. *The Road to Disunion: Secessionists at Bay, 1776–1854*. New York: Oxford University Press, 1990.

Gunderson, Robert Gray. *The Log-Cabin Campaign*. Lexington: University of Kentucky Press, 1957.

———. *Old Gentleman's Convention: The Washington Peace Conference of 1861*. Madison: University of Wisconsin Press, 1961.

Harris, Bill. *The First Ladies Fact Book*. New York: Black Dog and Leventhal, 2005.

Healy, Diana Dixon. *America's Vice-Presidents: Our First Forty-three Vice-Presidents and How They Got to Be Number Two*. New York: Atheneum, 1984.

Hickey, Donald R. *The War of 1812: A Forgotten Conflict*. Champaign: University of Illinois Press, 1995.

Hofstadter, Richard. *The American Political Tradition*. New York: Knopf, 1989.

Holt, Michael F. *The Rise and Fall of the American Whig Party: Jacksonian*

Politics and the Onset of the Civil War. New York: Oxford University Press, 1999.

Howe, Daniel Walker. *What Hath God Wrought: The Transformation of America*. New York: Oxford University Press, 2007.

Israel, Fred, ed. *Taught to Lead: The Education of American Presidents*. Broomal, Pa.: Mason Crest, 2004.

Jones, Howard. *To the Webster-Ashburton Treaty: A Study in Anglo-American Relation, 1783–1843*. Chapel Hill: University of North Carolina Press, 1977.

Karabell, Zachary. *Chester Alan Arthur*. New York: Times Books, 2004.

Keller, Morton. *America's Three Regimes: A New Political History*. New York: Oxford University Press, 2007.

Kunhardt, Philip, Jr., Philip B. Kunhardt III, and Peter W. Kunhardt, eds. *The American President*. New York: Riverhead Books, 1999.

Lambert, Oscar Doane. *Presidential Politics in the United States, 1841–1844*. Durham, N.C.: Duke University Press, 1936.

Latner, Richard. "Andrew Jackson." In Henry A. Graff, ed. *The Presidents: A Reference History*. New York: Macmillan, 1997.

Leahy, Christopher. "Torn Between Family and Politics: John Tyler's Struggle for Balance." *Virginia Magazine of History and Biography* 114 (August 2006), pp. 322–55.

Malenson, Philip H. *The Secret Service*. New York: Carroll and Graf, 2005.

Marx, Rudolph. *The Health of the Presidents*. New York: G. P. Putnam's Sons, 1960.

McCormick, Richard P. "John Tyler." In Henry F. Graff, ed. *The Presidents: A Reference History*, New York: Macmillan, 1997.

McPherson, James M. *Battle Cry of Freedom: The Civil War Era*. New York: Oxford University Press, 1988.

Merk, Frederick, with the collaboration of Lois Banner Merk. *Fruits of Propaganda in the Tyler Administration*. Cambridge, Mass.: Harvard University Press, 1971.

———. *Slavery and the Annexation of Texas*. New York: Knopf, 1972.

Miller, Nathan. *Star-Spangled Men: America's Ten Worst Presidents*. New York: Scribner-Touchstone, 1999.

Monroe, Dan. *The Republican Vision of John Tyler*. College Station: Texas A&M University Press, 2003.

———. "Lincoln the Dwarf: Lyon Gardiner Tyler's War on the Mythical Lincoln." *Journal of the Abraham Lincoln Association*, vol. 24, no. 1, pp. 32–42.

Morgan, Robert J. *A Whig Embattled: The Presidency under John Tyler*. Lincoln: University of Nebraska Press, 1954.

Moser, Harold D. *John Tyler: A Bibliography*. Westport, Conn.: Greenwood Publishing Group, 2001.

Nevins, Allan, ed. *The Diary of Philip Hone, 1828–1851.* New York: Macmillan, 1952.

———. *The Diary of John Quincy Adams, 1794–1845.* New York: Charles Scribner's Sons, 1951.

Peterson, Merrill D. *The Great Triumvirate: Webster, Clay, and Calhoun.* New York: Oxford University Press, 1988.

Peterson, Norma Lois. *The Presidencies of William Henry Harrison and John Tyler.* Lawrence: University Press of Kansas, 1989.

Remini, Robert V. *Andrew Jackson and the Course of American Democracy.* New York: Harper & Row, 1984.

———. *Andrew Jackson and the Course of American Freedom, 1822–1832.* New York: Harper & Row, 1981.

———. *Daniel Webster: The Man and His Time.* New York: Norton, 1997.

———. *The Election of Andrew Jackson.* Philadelphia: Lippincott, 1963.

———. *Henry Clay: Statesman for the Union.* New York: Norton, 1991.

———. *John Quincy Adams.* New York: Times Books, 2002.

Richardson, James D., ed. *A Compilation of the Messages and Papers of the Presidents.* Vol. 4, pt. 2, "John Tyler." Charleston, S.C.: BiblioBazaar, 2006.

Riddings, William J., Jr., and Stuart B. McIver. *Rating the Presidents: A Ranking of U.S. Leaders, from the Great and Honorable to the Dishonest and Incompetent.* Secaucus, N.J.: Carol Publishing Group, 1997.

Schlesinger, Arthur M., Jr. *The Cycles of History.* New York: Houghton Mifflin, 1999.

———. *The Imperial Presidency.* Boston: Houghton Mifflin, 1973.

Seager, Robert II. *And Tyler Too: A Biography of John and Julia Gardiner Tyler.* New York: McGraw-Hill, 1963.

———. *The Papers of Henry Clay,* vol. 9. Lexington: University Press of Kentucky, 1988.

Seigenthaler, John. *James K. Polk.* New York: Times Books, 2003.

Sellers, Charles G. "Election of 1844." In Fred L. Israel and Arthur M. Schlesinger, Jr., eds. *History of American Presidential Elections, 1789–1968.* New York: Chelsea House, 2001.

Shelley, Fred, ed. "The Vice President Receives Bad News in Williamsburg: A Letter of James Lyons to John Tyler." *Virginia Magazine of History and Biography* 76 (July 1968), pp. 337–39.

Sibley, Joel H. *Storm Over Texas: The Annexation Controversy and the Road to Civil War.* New York: Oxford University Press, 2005.

Silva, Ruth. *Presidential Succession.* New York: Greenwood Press, 1968.

Skidmore, Max J. *After the White House: Former Presidents as Private Citizens.* New York: Palgrave Macmillan, 2004.

Smith, Page. *The Nation Comes of Age: A People's History of the Ante-Bellum Years.* New York: McGraw-Hill, 1981.

Stathis, Stephan W. "John Tyler's Presidential Succession: A Reappraisal."
    Prologue 8 (Winter 1976), pp. 223–24.
Tolson, Jay. "The Ten Worst Presidents." *U.S. News & World Report*,
    February 26, 2007.
Truman, Margaret. *Where the Buck Stops: The Personal and Private Writ-
    ings of Harry S. Truman*. New York: Warner Books, 1989.
Tyler, Lyon G. *The Letters and Times of the Tylers*. 3 volumes. Richmond,
    Va.: Whittet & Shepperson, 1884, 1885, 1886.
Van Deusen, Glyndon G. *The Jacksonian Era, 1828–1846*. New York:
    Harper & Row, 1959.
Wead, Doug. *All the Presidents' Children*. New York: Atria Books, 2003.
Widmer, Ted. *Martin Van Buren*. New York: Times Books, 2005.
Wilentz, Sean. *Andrew Jackson*. New York: Times Books, 2005.
———. *The Rise of American Democracy: Jefferson to Lincoln*. New York:
    Norton, 2005.
Young, Donald A. *American Roulette: The History and Dilemma of the
    Vice Presidency*. New York: Viking, 1974.
Young, James Sterling. *The Washington Community: 1800–1828*. New
    York: Columbia University Press, 1966.

Acknowledgments

The book may be small but my debts are large. First, my thanks to those historians whose excellent work made my job easier: Edward Crapol, author of the best current study of Tyler's presidency; Norma Lois Peterson, whose survey of the Harrison-Tyler years belongs on every historian's bookshelf; the late Robert Seager II, who gave us *And Tyler Too*, a wonderfully readable introduction to the Tyler-Gardiner families; and Robert V. Remini, master biographer of Jackson, Clay, and Webster—his books epitomize the union of the historian and the artist.

I regret that Arthur M. Schlesinger, Jr., died before the completion of this work. Like many historians, I was introduced to the Jackson, Roosevelt, and Kennedy presidencies through his magisterial work, and I'm proud to be included in a series that bears his name. Sean Wilentz, the current editor, read the manuscript and gave me the benefit of his extraordinary knowledge of nineteenth-century American politics. Working with Times Books senior editor Robin Dennis has been a great pleasure. She is truly an amazing practitioner of a vanishing art, and every page of this book was improved by her hard work. Others at Times Books deserve acknowledgment: Jane Elias is a meticulous copy editor, Chris O'Connell skillfully oversaw production, and Paul Golob is a first-rate editorial director who runs an extraordinarily efficient and supportive operation. John Wright, my literary agent, once again proved indispensable.

Last but far from least there's Gail. For thirty-five years she's shared this writer's life and I wish to renew our contract: "If you're feeling fancy free, come wander through the world with me and every day will be a lovely day. As long as love still wears a smile, I know that we'll be two for the road, and that's a long, long while."

Index

ABOUT THE AUTHOR

GARY MAY is a professor of history at the University of Delaware. The author of three books, including the critically acclaimed *The Informant: The FBI, the Ku Klux Klan, and the Murder of Viola Liuzzo*, he lives in Newark, Delaware.